CONVERSATIONS WITH SHELDON

WILMON H. SHELDON
Sheldon Clark Professor Emeritus of Philosophy

(Yale *Alumni* Magazine, 1974;
Photo by Keri Keating)

Conversations
with Sheldon

by

JOHN MacPARTLAND

PHILOSOPHICAL LIBRARY

New York

To

NANCY *and* ANNE

Copyright, 1976, by Philosophical Library, Inc.,
15 East 40 Street, New York, N.Y. 10016
All rights reserved

Library of Congress Catalog Card No. 75-41648
SBN 8022-2179-3

MANUFACTURED IN THE UNITED STATES OF AMERICA

Preface

We might have missed one or two sessions over a five year span, perhaps. Otherwise, I have been meeting once a week with Professor Sheldon ever since I was a grad student in his metaphysics class in '38. The first conversation presented here will further orient you to the rest of our most recent ones. Sheldon says: "In recommending our conversations, if put into a book, the book won't be orderly, not logical. One of us gets an idea and he expresses it. But this is warmer, more personal; there is more feeling. These conversations have more breadth and are a more humane treatment of these topics."

What topics? Anything from nothing to the existential act that makes each thing be; from death to immortality; from the fall of man to the fall of Vietnam; the family, human and Divine; Ms., present-day youth, and the Trinity —the thread running through our discussions; two different worlds: Thomism and Modern Thought; faith and reason, philosophy, religion, and present-day science: the value of the dominant modern concept of energy; life, how to enjoy it *both* now *and* forever.

At 100, Sheldon might not be—"so far"—the oldest philosopher who ever lived, perhaps, but he is the oldest living Yale philosopher, to be sure. These conversations present the spirit and most recent developments of what he now calls his "Both-And Philosophy." I take notes on each session, type them up during the week, give them to him when I come in, and take back the previous report. These reports are presented to you here.

J. M.

OCTOBER 7, '72

Today I brought in my annual bunch of sea-gull feathers which I collect at the beach. Sheldon used to gather them in at Nantucket during the summer for his annual supply of pipe cleaners. He takes a pipe after breakfast—"the best physic"—one after lunch, at mid-afternoon, and after dinner. When his office was on campus, our dear friend, Connie Johns used to say he could smell the aroma of Edgeworth down at the Temple Street Gate. In those days he used to keep his door wide open. When I came in about 10:30, I knocked, passed greetings, went over to the chair at the left of his desk, and sat down. He is usually writing out checks to the various "begging societies." He liked to get off any business early. Then he was free to devote the rest of the day to his queen. He puffed away on his pipe until he finished this job. Then he opened up his upper left-hand desk drawer, and gave me a cigar. Many of them had been drying out there all summer. He used to get them at the meetings of the Ivy League philosophy professors at Columbia. They were mild, Havana tobacco, whereas I smoke strong Connecticut tobacco. However, I always accepted the cigar, and, if I felt up to it, I smoked it then. Otherwise, it usually disintegrated in my pocket by the time I reached home anyway. After I finished smoking the cigar, Sheldon would put it in his pipe and smoke the butt. He used to make a bon-fire of all the matches on his ash tray at the 3:30 pipe. I happened to witness one of these rituals when I came in one day by chance and saw him sitting behind the blaze. In his younger days—before he was ninety—when his fingers were a bit more nimble, he had a skillful way of shifting a partly burning match between his thumb and forefinger, from hand to hand, so that the match would burn out without singing his fingers. One

1

day, when I was a grad student, I came into his office after a seminar, and saw him performing his match trick. We had been discussing Hume on causality. Since the flame was passing from one match to another, I asked if he might not be experimenting to discover the causal tie. Although I did not know him very well then, it was a good question, because inclusiveness is the basic value of his philosophy and life—no divorce between them. Today he calls this his "both-and" philosophy. He was, then, doing the match trick for experimental purposes and also for the fun of it. That is why one of his favorite subjects is play, and he often refers to his friend, J. E. Boodin's last chapter entitled "The Divine Laughter." Sheldon says: "The Lord Himself plays in what He creates. That is why He is supreme bliss. Heaven is a place of joy. Play is not one motive among others. It is a joy in itself, and religion should stress its value more, whereas it has treated the value of play as trivial."

When I sat down to discuss with him today, he did not offer me a cigar, but he said, "I have something for you, John." He gave me a list of recently published philosophical books. I glanced at the list, and the first two titles were: *Understanding Understanding*, *Semantic Analysis*, etc.

He said, "These titles show how much philosophy has degenerated. There is no philosophy. They tell you how to be a philosopher. All analytic stuff. They are just a study of language. Obscurity is to be feared in any philosophical writing. That has given rise to this 'how to be clear'." Then he traced the retreat into the self of these logical analyses which are just concerned with how to think.

He continued, "I love pecan pie. If I say it tastes good, my analytic friend says, 'Give me a definition of good'. If I say my whiskey is good, I don't mean it is perfectly good. But they go to extremes and ask: What do you mean?"

In short, the quest for meaning has taken over philosophy. Fortunately, however, no matter how much they squeeze it, as Sheldon says, "There is no bad whiskey."

I showed him *L'Eternal Feminine* by Teilhard's Cajetan, Fr. DeLubac. I said it was a splendid job which made me rethink what we said when we discussed Teilhard's book on woman and also Soloviev's *Meaning of Love*.

We agreed that it is necessary to distinguish between female and feminine. Female-sex. Feminine is the way, we said, the cosmos dresses itself up in woman to lure man out of his ego back to God. That synthesizes Teilhard and Soloviev.

For them and for us, would there be "open marriage"? To another man or woman, no. To God? Yes. Teilhard insists on it. Moreover, propagation of the species is secondary to love "eternally and forever."

Sheldon said, "Lure. That is a power all women have, and men don't have it. That is a profound idea."

He ought to know. Lure was a big category in his book with that forbidding title *Sex and Salvation*. Mysterious woman just beckons you to come. In keeping with what he said there, I replied, "Woman lures man. He can either misinterpret her lure and try to possess her—*eros*—perhaps she is to blame herself for his misinterpretation. Or her lure can lead him to divine love: agapé."

Sheldon said: "Agapé is warm, friendly, real love, feeling the beauty of it. You might say all women have beauty, femininity. Woman is the disciple of beauty. When lure is merely physical, the beauty of it is missed. Too often her lure is interpreted as merely an offer to satisfy your organ of reproduction."

I said that many of the T.V. exposures of lure associate it exclusively with a gone wrong view of sex. Just a few nights ago there was a one minute quickie which showed the back of a girl, just her flowing hair. The man talking to her spoke just one sentence: "Are you going to tell your husband you are cheating on him?" She answers with one sentence: "For my lure, I use (brand name) hair spray." Judging from the prevalence of this type of thing, one could gather enough evidence to show there is an organized conspiracy against morality for the institution of another way of life.

We agreed that normally woman is not interested in sex

as such, but agapé—the eternal element comes through. This also makes her proud, hence she is jealous of other women. Now that Ms. thinks her role is to compete with men—Bobby Riggs vs. Billy Jean—She will become jealous of him.

We agreed that any exclusively negative view of the situation would be shortsighted. At least this good will perhaps come out of it. Some long standing inequities could be straightened out. To bring these out into the open is itself a good. For as Sheldon constantly says, God put evil here so that by overcoming it we would get better. No doubt, women's new freedom will be a crisis of growth—if she does not forget her role: "the eternal feminine leads us on," as the immortal poet says.

As Soloviev says: "For God His other—the cosmos—has the perfect image of femininity." He continues saying that God wants all of us to enjoy the beauty of heavenly bliss through woman. We might express the value of the feminine element by the following analogy: God is to the cosmos as woman is to man. In short, the feminine element is analogously connected with the divine. Consequently, if we empty the eternal out of the feminine, woman ceases to play her role. The elements of beauty, adoration, mystery, and romance that lure man have no basis. Woman becomes a sex-object.

Sheldon said, "As a matter of fact, God is as much mother as father. Sex is divine. Everyone has his eternal mate. Sex love is fundamental in human nature. It is good to live physically. Without sex we wouldn't be here."

During the discussion, I wrote down what Sheldon said about woman:

"In the Old Testament, woman is where evil first comes in. But evil was already present in man—love of power. . . .

"Woman stands for love. She helps persons. Doesn't care for principles. God is a person, not a principle. Christianity is a personal religion. . . . Women's Lib is going to the extreme now. It makes her compete with man. She should complement him, love him. . . . Physical energy becomes

4

spiritual energy as we get more love. That is why the body is beautiful, especially in woman. Woman stands for beauty; man for strength. Each should include the other. Power and love are united in the trinity of which the family is the analogous realization.

"Beauty is divine. It goes with the feminine side—love. ... Woman's great problem is to love other women. They are rivals for man's approval."

Rarely does he talk of himself, personally. But he said: "All I ask is did I get the truth. The central object of my life is to get the truth. Don't concentrate on the self. You are God's creature. He wants you to be as big as you can. Immortality is not persistence in the same stage. There is a steady increase of energy. The essence of personality is the ability to act. By thinking yourself well and allowing no contrary thoughts to enter, you make yourself well, so far."

When there are pretty ladies around, Sheldon gives them his undivided attention, and as a matter of fact it works the other way around, too. So, when I see Nancy, his daughter, and Anne, my wife, entering, I exit.

Sheldon had Jacques Rueff's *The Gods and the Kings* on the arm of his chair. He said he was looking forward to reading the last chapter, because he was not clear about Rueff's view. This is indeed a splendid work, and I am looking forward to hearing what he thinks of it.

As usual, Sheldon stressed the value of bodily life. "I hope you'll go forward with making a book on the blessed new life coming here on earth.... We don't have to believe in death.... In all the religious sects they believe in a separate after-life. It is only a bodily life here."

J: We have to get away from thinking in terms of mind and body. As you know right now I am working on energy, and I think this whole problem of death has to be repositioned in the framework of matter-energy. If my hypothesis is correct, the body should be conceived as a transformer. It is the means by which we transform our energy from its physical to its rational or spiritual state, from one state to another. Death is only the last stage in the recycling of the energy system that is you and I, the "climactic point," as Teilhard de Chardin calls it.

S: That is the right way. Energy has two forms. Spirit is present now. But you must put it in such a way that it is clear. If you put it in terms of energy, it will be hard to make clear to religion and science. Those in religion will say you are a materialist; those in science, an idealist.

J: If they think in these outmoded molds, I don't worry about that. That is their problem. Energy is neutral in regard to the states it assumes. That depends on the conditions in which it is realized. Any scientist should agree with that.

I pointed out that it is necessary to get rid of conceiving reality in fixed molds like mind-body, spirit-matter, this world-the next world. In the light of the dominant modern scientific outlook of energy systems, providing the rational energy system that is you and I is not itself fixed in a material mold, we can get rid of these bifurcations and the false problems they set up. The very nature of energy is involved in recycling. Science today knows how to convert solar energy into electricity for practically any purpose. You don't see electricity, as you don't see the state of rational energy into which the vitamins are transformed in the body. And when the rational energy system that is you or I no longer needs to make this transformation to advance, death works with life to remove these physical conditions.

And recycling can be understood by anyone today, because it is a household word, hence our scientific conclusions can be applied to these problems like death. This problem is still conceived in terms of a "billiard ball" conception of matter. I notice that Dr. Burns, for example, said that recycling money is the key to our recovery, not the *amount* of money. See, he is running into this thinking in molds among economists. You find it everywhere—unfortunately. Science already has the technical know-how to send up satellites over a city to condense solar energy into enough power to run a city—it is just a question of cost—yet these most important problems of our every-day lives travel around in a tiny lizzy—this is the main bifurcation that must be overcome. In other words, the energy crisis now comes down to "the net" cost, but it costs nothing to apply our knowledge to death.

December 10, '74

Sheldon finished Jacques Rueff's *The Kings and the Gods,* and I took it to return to the library. I offered to give him Castanenda's *A Separate Reality,* but he was not interested in reading, because he was rereading his own works "to see if I made any mistakes."

He said: "The best thing about Rueff's book is its emphasis on the individual. At the end he didn't connect his beliefs with what he was saying.

"To emphasize the individual is important. Reason and science don't do that. Reason deals with principles. But they need to be realized in the individual. Existence is always individual. That is the beauty of his book. That is why the love motive is fundamental. In man, every man tries to get what is good. The individual contains the good in the self, as is shown in our consciousness. We do what we like. We long to commit a sin, but we don't do it, because we want to go to heaven. There is no good without the individual. Science wouldn't be good if it were not true of individuals. Rueff's book does a good service. We have tended to forget the individual, because science emphasizes principles. ... Religion is concerned with the individual. Religion is a search of the individual for the best he can get. ... To write a book is what is done by our advanced thinkers. The emphasis is on principles. But religion emphasizes individuals. God is an individual; angels are individuals. If we go to hell, we suffer as individuals. You might say religion differs from science, because religion is concerned with the individual whereas science is concerned with principles. ... But still this is too exclusive. Religion isn't just individual. The principles govern the individual's behavior, too, even if the principle is just the Lord's will. There you have a productive duality. Polarity—two—the combination of the two gives a third, love."

J: Analogously, when hydrogen and oxygen combine, a new quality appears, the wetness of water.

S: Polarity is a trinitarian notion. My philosophy is the both-and philosophy. Include everything positive.

J: Applied to the problem of human death, death both leaves the remains and lets the energy system that is you or I through.

S: We must exclude the exclusively negative view of death. These exclusions cause all our trouble. Exclude exclusions.

J: When I mentioned your principle—exclude exclusions —to a bright fellow visiting Peter, he said: "Anyone who can come up with that ought to be worth listening to."[1].... People go to these barbaric wakes and say, "Doesn't he look peaceful?" But he is not there.

S: Remember poor Crito who was so concerned with how to bury Socrates. Socrates said to him: You may bury me any way you please, but make sure you get hold of me first.

J: Then he drank the hemlock. Today there is not even the prospect of a drink to loosen up these stiff affairs.

1. Hugo Black, 111.

9

DECEMBER 18, '74

Sheldon returned the report of the last session full of enthusiasm. He is always an inspiration.

He said: "The best thing you could write is a conversation. That is the way we get along. Real progress. I'm delighted with it. If it weren't for you my mind would be asleep. This is most likely to be read, because it doesn't require a lot of learning, is natural, proceeds step by step. It shows how ideas drift into the mind. The beauty of our conversations is that they are human. A new idea comes into our mind, just as the idea of the Trinity. I wish you could stress how Power comes first, after that the desire for knowledge—the physical sciences. Finally, the love motive entered—always present, but never outstanding."

I replied, "The Good Lord crowned your search for the Truth with this great love for the Trinity. My mind is geared more toward Leibniz's 'Divine Architect'."

Sheldon: "You are thinking of the scientific side. I'm thinking of the practical side."

Then he began to apply his own view of the trinity to the family, as he so often does: man, woman, child. But this time he did not speak of man (Power). "The trinity is empirically revealed to us in time, not all at once. God gave us time to see it. Woman has come nearer now to the recognition of her importance. But good often appears bad. The youth commit crimes. They don't realize they need intelligence, hence I quoted, as Jesus said: 'Unless you become as little children, you cannot enter the kingdom of heaven.' The youth stand out in public notice more than the adult. Although woman is outstanding, she doesn't seek notice with wild motives. Youth have self-exclusive motives. They have freedom; they don't know how to use it yet.... Freedom is all right if it doesn't prevent freedom.... But we must realize the good that youth has in it."

Then he pointed to the book I had and said, "What book is that?"

I showed him Broglie's *Matter and Light*. He, like many of these Frenchmen, is so clear. I read excerpts showing that the photon is completely transformed into the kinetic energy of the electron. "The inverse phenomenon again, the dematerialization of the corpuscle, is also believed to be possible."

I read many passages of this kind that show if death is located in the framework of matter-energy, the view that death is the end of the line is, to say the least, outmoded by present-day science. Of course, the "father of wave mechanics" might not agree with this application, but I am only verifying here a hypothesis which I have confirmed in the writing of many other scientists. Thus Gustave Fechner says that your life is a series of deaths, a "continual removal of envelopes." Your very birth is only "the death of your life in the placenta." As Leibniz says, death is a *metamorphosis,* and Teilhard follows in this line. Hence our view is that death is the transformation of energy from one state to another. The trouble is that people bifurcate death from the evolutionary process, blow it up into a false problem, stare at it in isolation, so that they commit suicide before they start.

I applied these points to the energy crisis and said that the exchange value of energy in terms of "livingry"—Fuller's term—is the proper point of view. Our economy is not based on gold, but energy. Moreover the most vital point he has the insight to stress—unusual today—intelligence is the essential ingredient in this exchange. Man is moving away from the fixed, from "deathage", as Fuller says. The microscopic, which depends mainly upon intelligence, shows it is now an essential ingredient in the macroscopic order. Consequently, the East is foolish if it thinks itself wealthy because it has oil, for without the science of the West their oil would be buried in the desert sand. If we're wise, our money should be put into *scientific research,* the develop-

11

ment of intelligence, not into war. By keeping ahead in *this* area, enemies keep away.

Sheldon said: "The hostile dualism between mind and matter must be overcome. We are overcoming it when we speak of mind-body as energy systems, as Boodin does. Man uses energy consciously. There is no gulf between consciousness and energy converted into the life of the mind. We exercise energy when we are conscious of exerting ourselves, when we try to do something. Our human energy is not just a physical process. It is effort, exertion. We try to make the world better, to solve the energy crisis. The whole point is the union of mind-body. Religion needs this point of view, because in the past it did separate the two. It was its own worst enemy."

I said: "On T.V., I watched a golf match yesterday in Florida, sponsored by Jackie Gleason. There was a threesome of Palmer, Nicklaus, and Murphy, plus a wide field. Murphy won. At the conclusion, Palmer and Nicklaus had their arms around each other as Palmer said words to the effect that often when they are in the same threesome, they are watching each other, but the third party wins. Analogously, the East and West must beware of Communism."

Anne packaged a bottle for the Professor for Christmas and revived our inscription on the first one: "A grad student's version of an apple for the teacher."

I gave Sheldon de Broglie's *Matter and Light* and urged him to read a splendid essay "Idealization and Reality." It agrees with his own view of the relation between chance and necessity, I said, and also with the Aristotelian view.

As usual I marked the place he is to begin, as he requests.

Sheldon said he has been reading over his *Agapology* where he expresses his view of this relation that has been misunderstood: "Chance is in perfect accord with reason. I don't give up reason. Chance has always been taken to deny logical necessity. But logical necessity implies what we consider chance. Properly understood chance is in accord with reason."

In introducing what he says in the following discourse, I should say that he has a deep, original, and unique approach to the understanding of present-day youth. It starts right from where we find youth today, in revolt from tradition. One must always remember Sheldon lives with the Trinity in historical orientation out of which he expresses these ideas. That is apt to sail right over my head at times if I do not pay careful attention to what he says, or if I take what he says out of this implied context. He began:

"What I would like to emphasize today is that we thinkers ought to realize the part youth plays in the progress of mankind. It is striking that the young are coming into public notice. And it is happening in the wrong way. The advance of a great good comes in from the side of evil. How did Christianity come in? By the crucifixion—evil. But Christ achieved victory which was taken as defeat. If the founder was killed, what can one expect from Christianity? But His crucifixion turned out to be the strongest base you could possibly imagine. A great good comes in as evil. This is a repeated fact in history. At first the scientists were regarded as the lowest form of belief by religion. So, think about what youth are doing. They have a gift they have never used. Youth has the great gift of freedom. Youth insists on it. Youth shows it by disobeying law. But understanding the meaning of law is important. The religious people regarded criminal acts as simply evil, but we must understand the deep underlying nature of youth. They need freedom in the right direction. Freedom is a Divine gift."

J: I agree with what you are saying, but many would regard it as wishful thinking. As Urban used to say: "Living in the future is a soft job."

S: I am glad you raised that objection. It makes me think. Intelligence is increasing. It is not just a hope youth will come around to learn to use freedom in the right way. Love is increasing, hence the universal desire for peace.

Of course, Sheldon wrote his *Agapology* to establish these points. No need to press and get sidetracked.

He continued, "The young people are full of evil—at present. If you judge solely by present appearances, the case seems hopeless. But look at history. Power (man) came first; women had no position, nor did children. But now woman is coming to realize her opportunity. Man, woman, child—the Trinity. All Christians ought to follow what I defend: power, reason, love. The love motive is most abused by the young. Evil develops to its worst before the turn begins. So with woman. She was most abused before she began to realize her splendid part. First, reason, man; second, freedom of woman—already come about. Third, we good Christians must believe love will be overcome at first. The young people feel their freedom in crimes. But they are not full of hate. As they grow, they become more intelligent—the second person.

How did intelligence develop? By hatred of ignorance. How will youth develop? By hating crime. This is the oppo-

14

site of a healthy desire for freedom. Youth don't want to be alone as never before."

J: You are right about that. Just listen to their tapes.

At this point the ladies entered.

As I type this over, perhaps I might make the following comment before giving you this report. As usual I think of what I should make clear after the session is over. There is no question about the fact that the Trinity gives us many beautiful insights, as indeed you are demonstrating. But for the protection of the value of reason, we should also emphasize that reason shows only the necessity of admitting a First Cause and the attributes following from it. But there is no reason God should be three, rather than two, four or one. Once He tells us He is three, then we get by reason's further use, as you are doing, many more insights by analogy. In short, there is no way to demonstrate rationally why God is three—even after He tells us He is three, because reason knows God only from His effects.

December 31, '74

Sheldon thanked me again for his Christmas present. He said, "You know what's good." I replied, "Thank Anne, she does, too." I reminded him of the time he was having a drink with a man of the cloth at the Grad Club and said, "If they had whiskey in those days, the Lord would have drunk it instead of wine."

Of Broglie's essay on chance and necessity which I left with him, he said, as I sat beside him, "His view is my own." I began to write immediately: "When it comes to details, it is chance. Chance is not against reason. The law of chance is all events are particular cases of a rule with slight variations. Chance goes with individuality. It is not irrational, because chance makes a better world. God gives His creation a matter of chance, because many chances reveal a necessary law. Chance loves its opposite, reason. Chance is generally taken to deny reason. No. It's got to be within this whole set of possibilities. Its got to consider the other. One matter of chance depends on all others."

I said that was also St. Thomas and Aristotle's view. St. Thomas, more being. Also, the romantic element.

I left de Broglie's book and urged him to read the beautiful essay on the value of intelligence in science, because I'm into the hook-up of intelligence and energy, and I would like the great man's comments.

Sheldon said, "A new idea has come to me. It is seen in the Trinity. Power is a good *in itself*. Power is the ability to do something. We all love acting on our own. That contains love. Power includes love and intelligence, because, if not rightly exercised, it destroys."

"Speaking of the misuse of power," I said: "Last summer there was a 'long, where's my ball' hitter playing behind Jack Boone and me. We would get on the green and call

16

him on, but he couldn't catch up. Finally, we were slowed down by a foursome of ladies on the next green. The powerful one strode up and said, "May I go through?" I replied, "There are ladies up front." He said, "I'll get through them." I answered: "Your game would improve if you stop trying to run around the course." He glared at me, put his ball down, and shot one right smack up against a tree. We then hit out to where he was looking around the vicinity for his ball. He put another one down and hit. Far out, but over in the woods on the other side. As he was going off the fairway in the distance, I hit, hooked it, and almost measured his length on the fairway. He turned around and started back towards me. I began to walk towards him—to apologize. Evidently, he had a power failure, because he stopped and shouted in the distance, "I'm going to report you." Then he turned around, walked into the woods, and that ended the incident. I was shaking in my golf shoes as I walked towards him."

Sheldon said, "We go to play golf and frustration is part of the game. Billy Phelps and I were playing one day, he missed a put, broke his putter on the green, got into his car, and drove away. We enjoy our power, don't want anything to check it, mentally or physically. . . . The trouble with Christian belief was that it did not seek happiness on earth. God gave us the physical world and our physical bodies are beautiful, hence the beauty of the medical profession."

J: That may be true of Christianity in the past, but not today. It has made progress, is alive, and grows. It is right not to confuse happiness—perfect happiness, our goal, with the bits we get now and then here. But I don't think in these molds of mind-body, mental-physical. I am interested in thinking and speaking in terms of energy systems."

S. "If you speak of energy, you will not be understood. The best way to persuade 'em is to speak in these terms. There is danger in the use of energy. I think we ought to speak in terms of spirit and body. They can't digest too much at once. The beauty of your work is that it is expressed in terms of conversation. You're bringing the issues

17

down to earth, not dictating as the religious sects do. When you educate a child, you use common sense terms, i.e., stones, water, etc. That is what Jesus did. No technical terms. He never appealed to learning, but common sense. That's how He converted people."

J. "I'm trying to correct false problems and errors caused mainly by speaking and thinking in these molds."

S. "Spirit and body mean a lot. Descend to the lower to rise to the higher. The trouble with philosophers is they appeal to a select group, but they should go far beyond that. Really, as I have said so often, it is a question of both-and."

J. "Of course, we agree. But it is also a question of getting them to think in terms of our scientific advance."

S. "But you have to speak in terms of spirit and flesh to show what these terms mean. Philosophers and scientists haven't done this. They speak in terms of matter and mind."

J. "That's my point. They shouldn't."

S. "You have to speak of evil. There's plenty of it. If you can show what evil is. . . . At bottom evil is exclusion, but it is not desirable to say that right off. What is love? Inclusion. The person we love we unite with. That's why love is both-and. But there wouldn't be joy in unity unless each had a value of its own. That's the difficulty of writing. To show these terms are exclusive. Your concept of energy is inclusive."

J: "Conceiving things in terms of energy systems is, as you should know, a key idea I got by synthesizing your old buddy, Boodin, and Teilhard's 'physicalism of the spirit.' Their idea updates the Aristotelian view in the light of the advance of present-day science. I find that materialism and idealism, and the Aristotelians, too, become exclusive mainly because they are boxed in by thinking in these molds. St. Thomas transcended all this in his view of *esse*, but that is such an esoteric view that present-day philosophers don't know what he is talking about. I am trying to work from the cosmic side of *esse*, but, as you are pointing out very well, there will be difficulties in trying to get this view across."

S. "Energy is inclusive. That's the beauty of it. Apply it

to particular points. In the old days power ruled. They didn't understand power is beautiful. Power is lost if it destroys others. Power is good if it is not exclusive, e.g., the power hitter on the golf course when he wants to play through everyone else. Yes, I was elated when it occurred to me power is beautiful. Isn't that why we worship God? He is Perfect Power. He allows us to do evil, so we can understand its power—joy, happiness goes with power."

J. "Power and intelligence or reason, we make no distinction between them here, are hooked up in energy. If it were not for the science of the West, the oil of the East would still be buried in the desert sands. The East would be very shortsighted if it thinks the exchange value of energy is gold, for science will find a way to recycle energy and the East will be left holding a bag of what "Bucky" Fuller calls 'death-age'."

S. Energy is power and it is beautiful. Power is misused when it destroys other power. The Kings and the Gods in the old days destroyed each other. They did not realize that side of it. Most Christians would say power is not good in itself, but only to create happiness. But power has a beauty of its own. Golf is a good illustration. It takes quite a while to play eighteen holes, and it takes power to hit a long drive, make a good approach, and put. The point is we don't try to defeat—just do a good job ourselves. In tennis they want to defeat someone. That's why you and I, who are devoted to a peaceful life, love to play golf.

J: Yes, Maritain pointed out that play is nearest to the contemplative. In the essay you are going to read by Broglie, he stresses the purely intellectual value of science, because without the natural joy of intellectual discovery, its practical value would be left waiting in the wings. Incidentally, last week I was in a foursome. One of the fellows stood on the tee. Just as he was about to swing a duck quacked. He swung and missed completely. He heard ducks quacking all around the course after that.

After some remarks on the beauty of the Yale course, he said: "Power goes wrong at first. Witness our youth—gone wrong at first. The same with woman. They want to be queens, many of them, have high political office, but there is more power in educating a child, because there is more instinctive knowledge. It's that old exclusive attitude."

J: We were invited for "potations" at the Wiedersheim's last week. I thought I would stir things up, so I presented a few of your points on man-woman. I quoted almost verbatim from your book; men are the creators, dreamers, planners. Women are practical; they are interested in the concrete, particular things of everyday life. A man goes to a drawer looking for a bottle opener. He pushes aside this utensil, that . . . the little woman goes over, picks it out, and holds it up under his nose.

I enjoyed the emotional outbursts of the ladies against me, but when the revolution comes it probably will be set off by some little thing like this, because the seeds are being dropped to make it total. One of the ladies said, "I'm not interested in the concrete details, my husband is." After Anne added a few blasts, I decided to have another Scotch: I agreed that if you approach a boy or girl from the rear today, you had better say, "Sir or madam—as the case might be." But I added, "Just ask 'em too take off their clothes, and you'll see the difference. . . . Can men bear children?" All your comebacks.

Sheldon said, "The good goes wrong at first, because the Lord wanted us to enjoy correcting evil. . . . That's the joy of love. You'll find plenty talking that way, because women are just waking up. The Christian Scientists agree that God is Father-Mother. I pray to Our Father-Mother God. Jesus did not teach that, because the world was not ready for it. He spoke in terms of man so his teaching would reach them."

J: You're probably right, but it is hard for us to know what man is ready for. However, I'm interested in the meaning and value of energy—to update thinking in the light of present-day science.

S: "There is no gulf, no separation between mind and body. Christianity made the gulf, but opened the way to unite the two. Mary Baker Eddy's healing. Spirit controls the body."

J: "We agree fundamentally, of course. But here you speak in terms of mind-body again—just what I'm trying to get away from."

S: "But that will appeal. It is important to dwell on it. When you come to the conclusion that bodily life is becoming more spiritual, you exclude the opposite. All I say is in our writing we want to appeal to these dualists, to show they should be understood. We have to speak in these terms. That's what you are doing. Put things gradually in a humanistic way."

Anne and Nancy entered. Anne wished the Professor a happy new year. Nancy said, "You have lived through two centuries, born in 1875 to 1975."

Sheldon replied, "I have lived through two centuries, but not for two centuries."

As I departed leaving them still talking, I said to myself, "*He* might make it."

JANUARY 20, '75

Today I brought in two books, one by Wilhelmsen, *The Metaphysics of Love*, an excellent work which mentions the Trinity at the outset, hence I thought Sheldon might be interested; the second by Mora on death. Sheldon's name is mentioned, and I thought he might like to see the quote.

Sheldon said, "the Trinity is the most fertile aspect of Christianity: Power, Reason, Love. But the Christian writers don't analyze the meaning of the Trinity, Yet, Christianity is the only religion that has made anything of it. What could be more interesting?"

I pointed out that he read Rahner's recent book on the Trinity, and, of course the early Church Fathers analyzed it along with St. Thomas's thorough treatment. But we agree that there is much more to be done, yet from the point of view of metaphysics, I confess I have little interest in it.

"Power first," he said. "Then reason, science. Finally, the meaning of love. . . . The essence of love is to promote the fullness of being, the fullness of the one we love. God wants us to become all possibilities in us. Woman wants the child to develop. Love=fullness of being of those we love. That requires reason. Love is not love without reason. That is the beauty of the Trinity: all parts are tied together.

"Proof of immortality is important. It is not just a matter of faith. Faith was treated all wrong in the past. Faith was taught as just sitting down, accepting; you believe, not trying to understand. Faith and reason did not go together. But they do."

I said that St. Thomas would agree with him that they do. That's why he wrote the Summas.

He said: "In my little book *Rational Religion*, I treat faith properly. Faith stimulates reason. Faith is a confident eye on final success even if you don't succeed. You don't fold your arms and say I believe. No. God gives us reason to use it. Faith is using reason in a spirit of confidence, but faith must be justified. It has not been understood by Christian sects. St. Thomas however, reasons about it."

"Yes," I replied, I'm glad you added that."

He continued. "Works have not been understood to include what must be taught. Faith without reason is dead. Faith is an attitude, but it must include bodily and mental works. Why did God give us intellect? So we could understand what he revealed."

"Let me add your famous expression 'So far'," I said.

He continued. "In my *Agapology* I show why he exists—ontological proof. I claim this is pure reason. Also, it comes through the value side—good—our experience. The good is self-realizing. If I think something is good, I would like to see it realized. There is a tendency to have it realized even if it fails. It comes to this: the good ought to be and, if nothing interferes, it will be. In my experience, if something is good and it is in my power, I realize it. If the good is self-realizing and God is good, then He is self-realizing. If He exists, He is self realized. Does He exist? Our experience confirms this. That is where we go behind Anselm. He assumes God's existence."

I said that he was going beyond St. Thomas, but including his proofs from experience, and Sheldon agreed.

If I understand Sheldon correctly, as I feel sure I do in this, he accepts St. Thomas's proofs which depart from our experience. He always did anyway. Then Sheldon goes beyond in the sense that he answers a further question: How did God get there? From his proofs, St. Thomas concludes to God as First Cause, Pure Act. That's as far as reason can go, or needs to, because it sees the necessity for admitting the First Cause is God.

FEBRUARY 4, '75

I brought in Ortega y Gasset's lectures on metaphysics and left them with Sheldon, because they are so clearly written. I understand he has a dynamic view of Aristotle, and I am suspicious he would throw light on the philosophical concept of energy, a very deep subject.

Sheldon stressed the importance of men in space. "Think of what they might discover. When the world gets settled, we'll come back to these problems. This takes us away from self-consciousness. People think man is God's central interest. Man is not the center of the universe. In our prayers we ought to include the work of these men. I do and I hope you will."

Sheldon spends much of his day in prayer. I said, "Teilhard would agree with you. He said, 'There is intelligent life on many planets.' Teilhard's Cosmic Christ has opened up this view, generally accepted by many scientists today, to religion. If the fundamental element out of which life evolves on another planet were not carbon, bodies there would not look like the ones we see here. Intelligence is an analogous concept. It does not need this body of the type man has here to operate. Consequently, when all the energy is "squeezed" out of the stiff at death, that is only the condition of the possibility of liberation from these human conditions, like the conversion of electrons into photons of light."

Sheldon said, "God helps those we pray for. Our attitude should be inclusive, not exclusive cosmic selfishness."

How about the touch, "comic selfishness?"

When I arrived, "the Professor" seemed to be dozing in his chair, but as I removed my coat he noted that I was late (about eight minutes), inquired about the weather, and began:

"With all this disturbance going on, what shall we do with youth? The reason for it? We give 'em freedom. The third stage is coming into prominence: love. They are being brought up. Does the teacher love his pupils? No, actually, but he is concerned about them. Youth is the object of love. We don't use the word in connection with them. We give them more freedom. Jesus said: 'Unless you become as little children, you shall not enter the kingdom of heaven.'

"So there is something about the youthful attitude that should be cultivated. The good almost always begins as bad. The Lord wants us to appreciate the value of the good. We must value youth. We give them the opportunity to learn. They don't know how to use it. They do what they please just to show their strength. Youth needs knowledge. They don't need opportunity. They had that. We gave them freedom without reason."

I said that I have been reading the *De Anima,* and Aristotle points out reason gives us power over the object, because we can reflect on it at will. By reason, then, youth can get the power to control freedom.

Sheldon: "They have to learn to use reason themselves, hence the teacher gives them problems. But teachers have a hard job today, because students are self-centered. Humanity went through the power stage—man was a tyrant. Now youth is going through it. Reason should come next. The teacher is trying to cultivate it, but they have freedom for its own sake. Now the second stage of the Trinity must come in.

"The love motive unites power and reason. Love is rational and, if we knew it, the greatest power on earth. It is self-realizing. Educate 'em to have knowledge."

J: Yes, Broglie would agree with you there, to be sure. However, today's youth have developed the power to stand up for their rights often at the expense of learning their duties to others with a lack of respect for the past—that will cost them much. But what did you think of Gasset's lectures on metaphysics?

S: He defines metaphysics as given with fact; it must deal with concrete facts. He is trying to refute idealism, but he identifies idealism with the Berkleyian type. That is unfair, e.g., Hegel.

J: I'm sorry I gave you that book, but he has another work that is a beautiful dynamic view of Aristotle. I thought the short sentences might be what you might like. Really, I was looking for Richard St. Victor on the Trinity for you, but everything is in Latin—you, too, are much more of a mystic than you are willing to admit.

S: The Trinity is a straightforward notion. Most religions rather think of it in terms of mystery, a relic of early times and forms of religion. Mystery and mystic go together.

J: I am curious to see how you would apply the trinity to the cosmos and its evolution.

Just for the fun of it, and to draw you out on the last subject mentioned above, what do you think of this? Man is on the threshold of advancing from the earthly to the cosmic stage now, let us say. If we conceive his advance in the light of Power, Love, and Reason, he has then passed through the first two. Power—The Old Testament. Love—The New Testament. Science—the third stage, now. Science has already shown he is a cosmic being by conceiving matter as energy. What remains is for all mankind to realize this, then man will know he is an energy system of cosmic dimensions. When he discovers who he is, he will be in a position to contact other intelligent life who will lead him further. When he knows who he is and what the cosmos is, he will be ready to appreciate the value of the Divine Plan and the Planner. If this analysis is correct, evolution in the light of the Trinity shows we are about now ready to contact other intelligent life, perhaps.

Today Sheldon seemed quite concerned that he might be going to lose one of his teeth. "How am I going to chew my steak"?

I simply said, "Use the other ones."

He looked at me as though I had made an astounding discovery.

I made no more of the matter at the time. But on the way out I said to Nancy that he seemed to be worried about losing a tooth.

She replied, "You would be, too, if you had never lost a tooth before."

FEBRUARY 18, '75

As I sat down, Sheldon said he had been thinking over an idea, but in his usual courteous way he quickly asked me if I had any new ideas. I asked him to read what I said in the last paragraph of the report I was giving him—I thought he might enjoy reading my application of the Trinity to our evolution for purposes of discussion.[1]

He read it and said, "Other ways might hasten the process—not to feel we have gone through Power and Love, with Reason as the final step. Historically, we have gone through Power, are in Reason, and are about to fulfill Love. Your way is less obvious—to say we went through the stage of love. Power, yes. We learned that Power is not enough. We resorted to Reason in science. Yet to come— we haven't developed it from the cosmic view. You can't say love has entered our region with all these wars. It is time for love to enter. It is now impossible to see it from Power, Reason, Love. Love is the final fulfillment of the good.

"Your stage of cosmic energy I perhaps do not understand. From a cosmic point of view as far as human progress goes—our lack of development of love is hindering our application of energy to history. Each nation is fighting other nations. That is holding up the development of energy. Your process is not revealed until we overcome the absence of love. Surely, it is worse to have this fighting going on—which absorbs our energy—than if we had peace to develop the cosmic point of view.

"Got to have love first before the normal Trinity can be realized. We in the West are beginning to lay less stress on power and more stress on love. We know power is good.

---

1. Report of Feb. 11, '75.

We in the West realized reason and it is necessary for progress. We have been taught by Christianity that love is beautiful. We have begun to realize that.

"You are looking at it from the scientific research point of view and it is right so far. But not so fundamental for our situation, as we can judge the constitution of the cosmos. Your point of view is correct, but for a more advanced stage than we are in. We need the development of love. Here in America we send our missionaries abroad to help poor blacks. What we want is to get rid of this fighting, and then we can get rid of the main obstacle. Then we can take your cosmic point of view. We haven't the intelligence to take it on yet."

J: If we get into the cosmic point of view....

S: I know what you are going to say....Your appeal is to reason. You are going through the road of reason more than I would.

J: This was just a hypothesis I used for experimental purposes, you remember. I tried to apply the Trinity to history. I see that it doesn't work. Why? Trying to explain x by x. We don't know the Trinity by reason to begin with, so it can't be much of a guide to history. I know many have tried this, and still hope to, but from this little experiment, you have successfully demolished my argument, and that's proof enough for me.

S: Love of the good is deeper than love of knowledge. The good is self realizing. Further development of love is necessary. You are going through the road of reason more than I would. The love motive is practical.

J: You mentioned that you had been contemplating on something.

S: It has been emphasized by your friend, Boodin. (He calls Boodin "my friend," because I like his cosmic point of view, although he was Sheldon's classmate.) Last chapter, *The Divine Laughter*. It appeals so much to our nature. How can we introduce it? Christianity is so serious.

J: Not the Catholic view. It is most joyful. The Jesuits, for example, are a happy band, most venturesome.

S: I know, but laughter seems to be superficial, so far anyway. That was the Puritan point of view.

J: But its gone, just listen to ministers on T.V.

S: I wish it had. Boodin thinks there is something in laughter that goes with evolution and reason. We should enjoy jokes just for fun. Laughter is fun, pure fun. It is contained in the Christian teaching of love for the young. The Puritans never had the opportunity of the joys of childhood. We enjoy a witty pun, a joke. Jesus did. Though He didn't teach it in those days. They thought laughter was turning from the good.

Does God laugh? Yes, He laughs with joy at the beauty of creation as He contemplates it. We should not laugh to scorn. Laughter means to enjoy with. We think laughter is trivial, but the trivial counts in influencing our attitude. Our infinite Lover, God, loves the least little thing as much as the greatest. His love is infinite. Space is infinitely divisible. The smallest thing in space is as big as the biggest thing.

Our sense of humor must not interfere with the love motive. When we laugh at someone, we make him feel cheap. That is wrong. There is the happy laughter of children, because they like something. What we like is good, so far; not if it hurts someone. Laughter is important and needed in its own way, because it helps make life good. Very few philosophers dwell on the value of humor.

———

As I type this out, I notice you said in passing that you perhaps do not understand the state "cosmic perspective." That is simply to include the discovery of present-day science, i.e., that matter is energy. We have discussed this with the help of Boodin and de Broglie. We get our energy from the sun, so does everything else; therefore, we are all energy systems, Boodin says, involved in the cosmic energy system. We have also discussed this in connection with Teilhard. I see no difficulty with this, because we are all involved in the cosmic evolutionary process which recycles our lives. The main point is that man is not merely an earthly being; he is a cosmic being. It outmodes a static outlook and locates him in history as a dynamic being. You also say that good is the most fundamental motive, but that depends on how one looks at it. There would be no love or good if they were not energized. One more point. Just because the physicist conceives energy by means of math does not mean that all energy is quantitative. That is Boodin's big point, there are different *kinds* of energy systems. There are stones, but also the rational form, men. Consequently, energy can be converted from one state to another as science demonstrates. I feel sure Aristotle would agree as would Teilhard, and, no doubt St. Thomas. Why not? These are simply facts. I am only trying to present the Divine Architect's plan from the point of view of philosophy of nature. Anyway I know one scientist, Dr. Mac-Mullen, who sympathizes with my intention.

FEBRUARY 25, '75

As I entered, Sheldon inquired about the weather, and before I was seated he said: "Puns. I wish I could recall some of those queer rhymes I made. Here is one:

> A famous New England preacher
> To a hen said, 'You beautiful creature'
> Whereupon, upon that
> She laid an egg in his hat
> And thus did Henry Ward Beecher"

J: I'll bet the Puritans enjoyed that one. Puns: you and Hegel. Remember how you used to go through the *Logic* and point out the twists in that dial-hectic.

S: All that fits in with the philosopher you admire, Boodin. His last chapter, "Divine Laughter." Let us dwell more on the fun motive as helping the deceptive attitude. Not scorn, laughing at, but laughing with.

J: Here is a book by a man with a deep knowledge of Thomism, Wilhelsen, "The Meaning of Love." I put a mark in the place where he takes up the Trinity in connection with Tillich.

S: Tillich was very popular with the Yale Divinity Students. When he spoke here, the hall was crowded.

J: I know. I went to the Terry Lectures. Yours, too.

S: He doesn't seem clear to me.

J: Well, I never read him. I'll leave it if you care to look at it.

Sheldon examined the book carefully, as usual, looking at the date of publication, etc.,—cautiously. He seems to say he won't swallow anything, takes his time as if he is letting you know that it is *his* time he is taking—not to be caught by the speed of this age. Indeed, the mistakes that are made in simple matters is frightening as if quantity controlled quality.

J: Here is another book by Chesterton, "Orthodoxy." I placed a book mark in the two pages where he talks most favorably about Unitarians and also on the Trinity: "It is not good for God to be alone."

S: He examined the book saying, "That's good." Then he sat back and said, "Conversation is good. We must not take churches on faith. My what a lot is written today rather than taken on authority! But your church has dwelt on authority."

J: Don't forget what St. Thomas said: "Authority is the weakest of all arguments."

S: The Catholic has kept it though. The Roman Catholic is at one extreme, the Unitarian at the other. Whatever the Catholic may teach, he emphasizes it a great deal. The Unitarian has no place for authority, except reason. How many devout men of the Christian sects pay attention to reason? Very few.

J: Perhaps they distinguish between religion and philosophy, as I do. Faith is the authority in religion; reason, in philosophy. St. Thomas wrote his Summas to show they support each other. No exclusive emphasis on faith in him.

S: Probably not. One of the best compliments I had on one of my books was by a Thomist who said I was very close to Thomism.

J: Perhaps I am as close to Unitarian views as you are to Thomism. The Unitarian would love St. Thomas, but unfortunately I find no connection at all between St. Thomas and modern thought. *Esse* is very difficult to see—takes a long time, hard going, so many pitfalls. And without *esse*, no St. Thomas.

S: Conversation is good. No book of any importance has stressed the value of it. Here there is nothing exclusive. This is a great novelty, because the writer is not just giving his own view. Both-and; your view and my view. And it is remarkable how deeply we agree. You a Roman Catholic, and I the exact opposite, a Unitarian. I no longer call myself a Unitarian except that I emphasize reason. Well, we enjoy what we are doing.

J: This is what the Aristotelian means by metaphysics —purely intellectual and speculative knowledge—for the fun of it.

S: We must emphasize the fun motive, hence Boodin's "Divine Laughter." Our emphasis on athletics has developed so much. Give each one full opportunity. I win one game; you win another in return. That's the sport motive. Very beautiful.

J: I can see you are starting another deduction of the Trinity.

S: Fun must be a loving fun. 'I've beaten you' is a joke. A happy rivalry, if rightly felt. We mustn't be unfair. No cheating. Rivalry. Honesty.... A real professional must love what he is doing in anything he does, or he can't be much good at it.

J: They are going overboard on woman's sports today. They are making women think they are liberated to compete with men. They are making women appear ridiculous. Some of the Amazons they show competing perhaps should have been men. Sports should take our minds off competition and the war attitude. Channel this energy into play, as you point out.

S: The outer world thrusts war on us. Islam does not cultivate everyday good. It cultivates mystical union apart from everyday life. Sport is deeply related to nature.

J: That is the typical American spirit or should be.

S: The individual is good in himself as well as in society. Democracy has gone overboard on the second aspect. The individual is good in himself. A woman's beauty is her beauty. Each has its own. Individual and social. Include both. Worship God as perfect in Himself and as creator. He loves Himself—is beautiful. And He does so with inclusion. Inclusion is love. We value this, that, and the other. Love is no better than intelligence. Intelligence is love. Reason loves its own work—is beautiful. The scientist is not supposed to consider beauty, but how one thing fits into another is beautiful in itself. That is where the Trinity comes in. He is not separate persons. Three in one: Power, Reason, Love.

J: Not separated persons, I should say.

S: For you the Trinity is just a dogma.

J: Yes. You live with it, but who can think it over as you just did? Very few, but you are speaking analogously, of course. You point out beautiful analogies everywhere.

S: It is beautiful as rational. Reason shows love is a necessity of being. We want to become intelligent, not sit back in faith. I bring this out in my *Rational Religion*. I'm not talking against faith. Faith stimulates us to investigate. Is it really true? Correct? Faith must not stop. It is a stimulus. Quite often we find out we don't know why. We're finite. We have to sit down and rest. We must enjoy every moment, hence sport. What a joyous life! Science is not fierce competition. There are new ideas, new mysteries. It is a joy to be a scientist. Play is a joy. It leads to love. The person we play with we help. We love to have him there, be fair to him.

MARCH 6, '75

S: Our discussions lead to the union of spirit and bodily life. Evolution leads to the immortality of spirit and body in this world.

J: I do not think in these molds. I think in terms of energy. Are you thinking about life on other planets perhaps?

S: Not merely. The teaching we are following is that immortality will be realized here on earth.

J: It could be, but not necessarily.

S: It is necessary. The teaching here is that we live longer here on earth. The Christian sects did not come to this, but Mary Baker Eddy was leading to it.

J: That may be true. Energy is neutral in regard to its states.

S: At present it is. Spirit and body are like man and wife —united in marital life. There is no gulf.

J: I agree. It is a good analogy.

S. Eventually, evolution will realize their union here on earth. That's my teaching.

J: Again you are talking in these molds. On other planets, because the substance from which life evolves could be different from here, energy there could be realized to live longer and in a different state from here. That depends on conditions.

S: That is all right, so far. But it is stopping progress. You ought to go further. Mind and body are two different things, but two in one. Jesus was an example of that. The Trinity is an example of that, not as hitherto understood, but as two in one. Reason is beautiful. The man who thinks he is just logical wouldn't think if he didn't love it. Power and reason are both love, if rightly understood. Freedom of the will means the gift of following what is lovely, not what is physically compelled. Freedom of the will is perfectly ra-

36

tional. Chance is not ultimate. It is merely the external appearance. There is always a reason why. I don't see how you can escape going on. It really comes back to the Trinity. It is rational, logical, necessary.

J: Man's immortality does not follow from this.

S: Of course he does not have it now. But if he realizes what the Trinity means he will in the long run, because there is no gap between power, reason, and love. In God they are one. In His creatures they share His nature. He creates us with this in mind.

J: God had His nature. We have ours. This sounds like a form of evolutionary pantheism. We don't know the Trinity by reason. We don't see the necessity for the Trinity in God. We know Him by analogy. Power, reason, and love are analogies from what we see here.

S: No. The Trinity is a religious dogma for you.

J: Yes, because reason takes us to the First Cause only from his effects. Everything else we know of Him is by analogy.

S: We have a fundamental difference here.

J: Yes, you are absolutely right.

S: The great difficulty is why God permits evil. The answer is so that we develop the power to overcome it.

J: That is the value of evolution.

S: Then you have to say eventually immortality will be realized on earth.

J: This does not have to be. God could end it anytime, or man could blow it up.

S: Everything points to it. I'm just a finite man and might make a mistake. But why did God bring in time. So that evil might be overcome. It takes time to recognize evil. There are more wars than before. Hence there is more love of peace.

J: Agreed.

S: But you are making an end of progress. It is of the nature of time not to stop. I don't accept Mary Baker Eddy's view because she denies matter. God made it to reveal the nature of spirit.

37

J: Here, under space-time conditions. Time has no independent status. Quantum physics and Aristotle agree here.

I have been reading in the *De Anima*. Aristotle says that reason, our power to think shows the end is the beginning of a new act. Both end and beginning. We solve a problem. We can go over it again. Rational energy can be recycled indefinitely. We do this every time we use the little word 'therefore'.

S: It can go on forever. We may go to sleep, but sooner or later we wake up. Our reasoning as we live here is finally fulfilled.

As I type this out, permit me to add that I think St. Thomas's view of analogy of proportionality might help to bring us together. It is the inclusive view, the both-and that is needed here. The qualities—power, reason, love, or any other—exist one way in God, another way in us. You said above, "In God they are one." Right. Why? Because He is an infinite *being*. In us they are split up. Why? Because we are finite *beings*. Therefore, being determines how the qualities are to be applied, not our reason. In other words, power, reason, and love have no existence in themselves. They have to be used analogously if they are to be understood properly.

As I was leaving, Nancy said, "Daddy is on a mayonnaise binge. He puts mayonnaise on everything."

I said, "Now I understand why he was especially bright. I thought it was just because you ladies entered, the old dog."

If I haven't made note of it before, let me say now that his graciousness with the ladies is indeed captivating. I have never yet seen him in want for the right, witty thing to say to loosen one up for a pleasant conversation. Well, that *Sex and Salvation*—what an awful title—is easily the best philosophical—deepest in metaphysical insights—job on woman I have ever read. And anyone can read it, because he has no peer in the use of the Anglo-Saxon word. "Big words are no good," he says. For confirmation of what I have just said—the relation of the sexes expressed in Anglo-Saxon words—just read the last four or five pages of his massive *God and Polarity*. He has not seen this comment, incidentally, although he has read everything else in these reports.

MARCH 11, '75

PREFACE

I went to see Sheldon this morning with a rather distasteful task in mind. Because he pressed me last time, I felt that perhaps I should press him. We usually don't do this, but it is good for a possible reader to know exactly where we stand, and I am far from being clear on his position myself. As we went along he kept saying there is "difference, but no opposition between us." However, from our last conversation, it is obvious that the differences are very fundamental indeed.

Sheldon is a man who has God's highest gift to the philosopher, a genuine love for the trinity, and he wants others to share his love for it. He has advanced from unity, to polarity, to the trinity. A few years ago after we finished writing a work, he said, "What shall we do now?" I replied, "You always wanted to write on the trinity. Perhaps we could go into it now." He said, "That will keep me alive."

However, these are conversations, not a treatise on the trinity, or anything else. When he opens his mouth I never know what is going to come out. I shall attempt to press him a bit this time, but after that the future will have to take care of itself.

I am interested in the problems of death and immortality, but I do enjoy the beautiful, practical insights he gets from his view as practical analogies for our daily lives, yet I am intentionally a Christian philosopher. From the discussions presented here, I have concluded that the trinity is not much of a guide to history, as indeed the reader will recall from a few conversations back when I attempted this experiment.

Sheldon began by saying that Brand Blanshard had come to see him and suggested that I might be interested in reading the work of this "kind hearted person" who was a "rationalist."

I suggested that Sheldon make any corrections he thought necessary in these reports, because it was becoming clear that they might be published. I pointed out that I took down what we say in long hand, and many times our conversation was ahead of what was being written. Sometimes, too, I am not sure that he hears me, and have to shout, not at him, but so that he hears.

He replied, "I don't have any corrections. I don't think you misrepresent what I said. I have much sympathy with these conversations.

"One point I might raise. In recommending our conversations, if put into a book, the book won't be orderly, not logical. One of us gets an idea, and we express it. But this is warmer, more personal; there is more feeling. These are good to put into a book, because they have breadth and a humanitarian attitude. This is a more humane treatment of these topics."

I spoke of the great interest in religion today. Sheldon said he received a book recently listing over 300 new sects. "Religion is becoming more universal," he said. Then "I have always admired St. Thomas's rational attitude. There are other things besides reason. You have it in the Trinity: Power, Reason, Love. The Unitarian talks against the Trinity."

I said I would like to sharpen up our views a bit for a possible reader and presented what I take to be St. Thomas's position on the Trinity, as follows:

"There are three distinct persons in the Trinity. Each one is God. The mystery of the Trinity is how can the same nature, God, be possessed by the Father, the same nature be the Son, that same nature be the Holy Spirit?"

Sheldon simply said, "I know."

I went over it again, slowly, emphasizing the words persons and mystery.

Sheldon said, "I try to point out there is no fundamental difference there. He means persons as a separate individual. It has come into a different meaning."

J: We say it means one thing, you, another.

S: You respect and love Jesus so much you make Him a separate individual. You use it your own way. You adore love so much you make it an individual person. God is all love. Each person is the whole of God.

We advanced to another point, and Sheldon said: "God gives a part of Himself to the stone. He has an infinite amount of it. Every individual thing sooner or later is identified with an infinitely small part of his creator."

J: I know everyone does it, but I don't like expressing metaphysical distinctions in terms of whole and part. The stone has its being one way; God has His being another way. That is the language of analogy.

S: Partial identity is analogy. You are other, but there is no contradiction between us. He does not give us reason as a part. He gives reason as a separate expression. It is His gift. We are separate from God. That is why we can do wrong.

J: This is a shady area. Color this brown.

S: Yes, this is a delicate area. But there is no fundamental difference between us.

J: To a person reading it. . . .

S: To the ordinary person reading it. . . . Certain ideas disappear from our memory. Everything we humans do is imperfect. But no one is any better. Let's get 'em down. I don't like feeling there is a contradiction. We seem to disagree on the surface. Individuality involves otherness. You say God makes you whole in yourself. But He gives the whole to you in an apparently separate expression. Where you have separation from God, you have evil. Remember He contains an infinite number of different individuals. The Trinity is imperfect for us human beings. Power is good if you don't destroy others. Reason is good if we don't make

42

mistakes. Love is misused by giving to the loved one something that will hurt him. But why did God make evil possible? To give us more power.

J: Yes, Teilhard speaks of evil in terms of our passivities. An athlete has to suffer through the training period to be any good. One of the main things we might differ on is the Mystery of the Trinity.

S: No. Two things can be the same and different. One and three at the same time.

J: One what?

S: Being. God.

J: Three what?

S: Three aspects, natures. That is really your view too.

J: Why three? God has more attributes than reason, power, and love.

S: They may be reduced to three.

J: Because faith, revelation tells us there are three. That is really your view, too.

At this point Nancy and Anne entered, and Nancy said, "He had beef stew for breakfast this morning."

As an appendix to our last discussion, I said that our view of analogy—which is really your view of both-and—might bring us close together. As I read over what you say here in your last long reply, my hope is still alive. You say: "The Trinity is imperfect for us human beings. Power is good if you don't destroy others. Reason is good if we don't make mistakes. Love is misused by giving the loved one something that will hurt him."

Right. That is what I mean by analogy. God has these attributes His way, because He is a perfect being. We have these attributes our way, because we are imperfect beings. That is what you said.

In short, so that these attributes will not be hypostatizations, we should conceive them in the light of the being who has them. This means that the Trinity is perfect in God and also imperfectly known by us. Indeed, you could accept this, and it leaves open the door for faith to tell us He is three, include Him in our conversations. Whatever we do must protect the life of the mind from being at the mercy of three absolutes, Power, Reason, and Love. Otherwise, that is, if these three become hypostatizations or absolutes, you lose both the being of God and the three persons.

MARCH 18, '75

J: Good morning, Professor.

S: John! You're early.

J: (Looking at the majestic grandfather clock, I saw that it was exactly 10:30.) 10:30, right on the button.

S: I'm concerned about your publishing your work on immortality and death. You used an argument showing the timelessness of reason, and this must not be lost.

J: Reason—the now of immortality. Yes, I think I have a new slant on this from the point of view of energy. But I'm more interested in our conversations right now, because, as you have pointed out, people are more interested in the informal. Last time we mentioned this great religious surge today. I've been wondering why. I wrote out a page on it.

S: Why this religious surge? A very good topic.

Then I read the following:

One of the basic values of energy is that it can be converted from one state, one system into another.

S: Yes, of course.

J: Because of T.V., mainly, everyone uses the expression "recycling of energy" as part of his everyday lingo. Whether we put it in terms of "recycling of energy" or in more scientific terms as the conversion or transformation of energy, they mean the same thing. The point is that the problem of pollution and the energy crisis have bridged the gap between science and our everyday lives. For example. . . .

S: Yes, we want concrete examples.

J: For example, in Conn. recently—last night on T.V., the news—the people learned that there was a bill in the legislature which, if it passes, would outlaw disposable containers. They showed packaged in disposable bottles—beer, for example. Those for the bill argue that its passage would help eliminate pollution; those against show how it would put thousands out of work whose jobs depend on recycling energy.

I had great difficulty in trying to get through to Sheldon on this, because his hearing could be better, and he pronounces job with a Boston born Harvard accent. After much shouting, he finally came up with what sounded like, "O, jōb." Moreover, he does not drink beer, hence did not understand disposable containers, nor has he seen T.V., never so far as I know. Finally, I said it is more difficult to explain the example than the point exemplified, so I said, "Forget it. Here's the main point: For Twentieth Century man science has already been taken off the shelf. What the scientist does in the lab gives us the know-how to transform energy. Consequently, since science studies the cosmos, it is no longer something out there, but part of our everyday lives."

S: The gulf between science and living has disappeared. Science is applying itself to everyday life. A big point. When my daughter plans my breakfast, she applies scientific knowledge—what food is good, as never before. Not *wholly*, of course. Scientists still do work the public knows nothing about. But there is a *whole* now. There was a gap before.

J: You equivocate too much for my taste, but let's get on with it. Our jobs.... Again we had a shouting contest —which disturbed the ladies; they thought we had come to blows. I said that our whole economy depended on new and better ways to recycle and transport energy. This also effects our foreign policy. If we can't get or import oil from the sands of Arabia, because of economic and political hasseling, or because of the deep ideological struggle for control of the world which is no doubt behind all this, the little man out in the country, even he has to pay more money for his gas. Indeed every man realizes today he is a little man dependent on an environment over which he has no control.

S: Man today is dependent, involves others. Isolation has gone by. We are dependent on opposing forces we can't control. This is the problem of evil. We feel it now as never before in history. Here religion comes in. Sounds Puritanical. We need the love motive. Formal religion, not much. They

said, "Save yourself. Obey the church, and it is enough."
The love motive was dark before.

J: We need the love motive—not as an empty formality,
however. We need it filled with the content of its direction
to the Ruler of the Universe. The religious revival means
man realizes his need for help. The Catholic Church calls
this help grace and has the sacraments which are the visible
signs he can get it. They show man has *Someone*, the Supreme *Being*, Architect of the Cosmos, to Whom he can
turn, instead of to the occult which he is also turning to now.

To continue. This recognition of man's dependence on the
cosmos is—in effect—making him realize his dependence
on the Divine Plan.

S: Really it is, but I doubt if he realizes it.

J: I'm only saying this dependence implies his recognition, otherwise he wouldn't be turning to religion.

To continue: Everything is coming together, hence this
great religious revival.

S: Big sentence. Put it in caps. In a clash of opposition or
in loving union, the world is no longer a place of separation.
The nations are coming together in fights or in loving union
or both. Yes, the world is one—a troubled one, more than a
comfortable one, but that is as it should be. At first in
fights; gradually in union. This is a union of opposites where
opposite means opposed——oppose it, or a loving union.
As in a happy marriage, there is a union of opposites—man
and woman. We want to be one happy family. The world is
a unity in battles, or in peaceful cooperation; the world is
coming to be one.

To continue; I said, "Man is returning to the time nature
depended on God, and man recognized his dependence. Now
he is recognizing his dependence on a new level—in terms of
energy. The problems of pollution and the energy crisis have
an ultimate value. They are recycling his energy on a new
level."

S: The God of early religions helped, but He did not care
about others. Just do what He says. This is one of the evils
of sects. You got to do it this way. You got to be baptized

47

or go to hell. They don't say that now. Both-and. You and me together. For example, in the family, man had all to say, the wife nothing to say.

J: Now dad is the silent partner with the arrival of Ms. Man has grown up. He used to be an earthly child. Now he is a "cosmic Child," in Teilhard's words. Religion must and should adjust to the times; nothing wrong in this. Each sect believes it has the truth, and it should; otherwise it has no reason to be. And it should have its own rules. But today all of them realize they are working toward the same goal— the Truth, hence there is *rapprochement* today. Things are coming together.

To continue. If our analysis is correct, based on the open-end view of science, everything is coming together, so that man can advance out into the cosmos. He is getting ready to surge forward, perhaps to contact other intelligent life. As Teilhard says, man is a cosmic child. He should not nail himself down to a value scheme based on things of this earth. Religion, too, should take on this perspective—the Cosmic Christ.

S: All inclusion. Before man was interested only in his own advance. We should encourage these brave men going out beyond to land on other planets; a great point you are bringing out.

Good always takes a bad form at first. Why did God permit evil? So that we would have great joy in overcoming it. The first reaction against evil is another evil, e.g., the opposition between capital and labor. The revolt against capitalism went to the other extreme. Labor now has us in its fist. But we will settle down.

The same idea comes out in all our discussions. Both-And. Difference and unity.

J: Right. You have made a great discovery in your both-and philosophy. I agree with you on this. But I differ— both-and—from you on the way to use it or see it. It should not be used to bring about a mélange, all things mixed together. That is confusion. This causes more confusion, equivocation, intellectual confusion.

Again we come back to the same point. Both-and should be based on the proportion of *esse* to essence. Both God and man are alike as far as they have being, and they differ in the way they have it. Things must be seen in their proper place; we need order—metaphysics—today. As you say, difference and unity, but "Distinguer pour Unir."

Anne and Nancy entered and, as usual, Sheldon brightened up to greet them. Nancy said: "He had corned beef and cabbage for breakfast this morning in honor of St. Patrick's day."

I left them talking and I thought back to my days in the grad school when he wore a kelly green tie to class.

Let me propose this for consideration during Holy Week.

As I said last time, the Good Lord has blessed your work with His great gift of love for the Trinity. But you don't want people to misunderstand what you say about it. Knowing you, I feel you don't want them to think you deny God the right to His own being or to know His mysteries which you and I as finite beings cannot know. But, if this is your view, you should make it very clear. At present, however, from what you say, I don't even know the mysteries in you.

When the air has been cleared, the great value of your work will appear. For you use reason to show there is no contradiction in the trinity. Good. Also, you are using reason to show its great practical value in our everyday lives. Good. I don't know anyone who is doing this more beautifully. But far enough. You should also make clear that this is not intended to be a proof of the intimate life of God. Both-and.

In the last analysis it comes to this. If you mean to say God is realizing His being in the world—and the same holds for the Trinity—then, of course, that *excludes* my view. Moreover, if you mean to say we can know the intimate life of God, His mysteries, the same conclusion follows. These are Yes *or* No answers. Happy Easter, Professor.

49

MARCH 25, '75

When I entered, Sheldon asked about the weather, because in many respects he was an outdoor man. I said it was so good I intended to play golf. He replied that golf was one of the Lord's best gifts to humanity, because "you can do it alone." Then he graciously turned to my work on immortality and asked how I was doing. I said I would like to repeat the essence of my argument to get his comments.

The argument begins by contrasting material and immaterial activity. Material activity is transitive. It goes out. It ends in otherness. You divide things up; or, you join things together. These are Aristotle and St. Thomas's examples, but they did not call transitive activity production of otherness.

By contrast, immaterial activity ends in the opposite way, as John Wild points out. *The* type of immaterial activity is imminent. I call this a conquest of otherness. Why? because the mind returns to itself, recycles its energy. That is to know. The otherness between subject and object is overcome in the knowledge act.

Conclusion: since the mind acts by overcoming otherness, its very nature must be a conquest of otherness, for we know what a thing is from what it does. *Therefore,* once the mind exists, it is indestructible, hence immortal.

Sheldon commented: "The mind is essential to man. He is immortal, because the mind sees things as a whole in a timeless way. This should persuade any intelligent person. What you say here is very simple."

Sheldon has captured the essence of the argument and represented it in terms of time. Perhaps it should be pointed out that the word simple might be misunderstood here. He means that the argument was simply expressed, not that the subject matter is not complex. In fact the difficulty here is that so much knowledge is presupposed about the transcen-

50

dental unity of being—which is foreign to present-day thought—that I am trying to recast the argument in terms of language of today, recycling energy, with the hope that at least the reasoning can be made clear, and then one can pick up what is presupposed later. Thus:

As Aristotle points out in the *De Anima*, in an imminent act, the end is the beginning of a new act. For example, you solve a problem, but your solution can be the point of departure for a new go-round. This is to say rational energy can be recycled indefinitely, because its very nature is to conquer otherness. Analogously, the very nature of existence is to conquer non-being. Consequently, once reason exists, you can no more separate existence from it than you can separate the end from the beginning in its manner of operation.

Let me recast the argument again from the point of view of the rational energy system itself, because the problem is to show it is able to hold on to the act of existence. As Aristotle says, at will we can turn reason off or on indefinitely, because it is one system. It can't be split into parts, and the system can't be separated from itself, hence it is of the very nature of rational energy to exist in this circle. Therefore, once existence is contained in the rational energy system that is you or I, we live forever.

To express this in terms of a concrete analogy. There are no holes through which existence can leak out of a rational energy system, because it is a conquest of otherness; therefore to be a man and to be immortal is one and the same.

These arguments have very deep ontic roots, because they are based on the transcendental unity of being and analogy. Without writing a chapter on these, let us simply say there is no part of existence that is not existence, hence existence is transcendentally one. But each thing holds existence in its own way; that is to say, it is analogous. Thus the moth holds existence so long as it does not get too near the flame. But man, once he exists, is able to hold existence forever, because there is no otherness in the rational energy system.

When rational energy is turned around—recycled—to face

the knower, it both reveals its own sufficiency and immortality. It shows its self-sufficiency, because it simply follows its own principle, that of the law of non-contradiction on which all rational conclusions is based. And it shows that an energy system which operates by conquering otherness must live forever, otherwise it would be contradictory. Hence the characteristic act of the life of the mind is a total intussusception.

Sheldon said, "The mind sees the whole first. That is a fundamental contrast between mind and body. The mind sees something at once which, if we stop to apply it, we see realized in some physical process. We see at once what is coming. We leap over time. That is what genius consists in. It sees the truth of an idea, and it knows we should come to it—sees by a non-temporal insight. The mind leaps over time. It knows. It is timeless. Genius is timeless. The mind leaping over time is the backbone of the whole proof for immortality."

I said, "You always come up with a new slant on the matter."

And his usual gracious reply, "You lead up to it so it would occur."

Perhaps in this particular case, up to a point, but even here the idea of leaping over time and genius never entered my mind. Indeed, I have heard him talk for ten or fifteen minutes on a subject, especially during these past four or five years more than before, coming up with one new idea after another like the two above. Then he shuts himself off by thanking me for the ideas. Upon reflection, the main things I can recall about genius are in terms of I.Q. measurement, their eccentricities, or that they were mainly musicians, mathematicians, or chess players—mathematicians gone wrong. It was quite refreshing to find a philosopher with first hand knowledge of the subject putting his finger on an essential trait.

Let us conclude on a forward looking note. When Teilhard de Chardin said man is a "cosmic child", he pointed out what 21st Century man will be. As Sheldon points out here, man is "leaping over time." The old barriers between the temporal and the eternal are being overcome by science today, because science is part of daily life. This means that man today is discovering that the Divine Architect's Plan was not written in the sky just for the angels to see.

We might bring this out in the light of this analogy which we need not develop here. You can take it for what it is worth. Pollution is to the Energy Crisis as death is to a crisis of growth. The common denominator for all the analogates here is the recycling of energy. If the analogy has value, it means our new knowledge of the first pair could lead us to a better understanding of the second pair.

Pollution and the energy crisis are perhaps our most pressing problems today. But we are learning that by recycling pollution, waste tin cans into other substances, for example, we help solve the energy crisis. Analogously, if death did not recycle human energy, there could be no remains. Is this not helping us see death is a crisis of growth? I could say much more on this. But the main point is that as man advances out into the cosmos, he is learning by the problems he is encountering more about his own destiny. Evolution is only the Divine Plan in action.

If people would stop locating death in a framework of matter that was outmoded hundreds of years ago, they could see that death is not the end of the line. For example, who has even posed this problem of the remains? I'd like to know. They still think of the body as a stuff whereas it is made up of electrons. Well, 21st century man will have a better understanding of these matters. There is absolutely no need right now on the basis of present-day science to face death—that's it, they say—as a Stoic going to his doom. They should face it as a growth, a transformation, as Christianity has always taught, and present-day science confirms in its view of matter as energy.

APRIL 2, '75

It is rather difficult to record the *tête-à-tête* conversation we had last time, so I am not trying to do that here. I shall discuss just the important point.

As St. Thomas says, devoting several chapters to the defense of the view that Christ is God, we don't pretend to understand perfectly what comes to us from Holy Writ.[1] To take another example from our discussions, I have said that reason cannot show why there are 3 rather than 2, 5, or 10 in God. But St. Thomas defends the logic of our belief that Christ is God quite satisfactorily, and it might be good to know the general Catholic view, and why I like this logic although Catholics themselves differ on these matters. There is great levity in the Catholic view. Duns Scotus, as you perhaps know better than I, didn't accept St. Thomas's view of analogy which I follow, for example, as did Aristotle before him.[2]

Some years ago, when you were writing on play, I quoted to you from St. John: "In the beginning was the Word, and the Word was with God, and the Word was God. . . ." Sacred writers identify Christ and the Word, and the passage goes on to say that Christ was with His Father "playing before Him when He set the foundations of the world . . . and His delight was to be with the children of men." In short, according to Scripture, Christ was God before He became man.[3]

Christ always claimed He was God, and He cannot be properly evaluated apart from that claim. His apostles re-

---

1. *S. C. G.*, vol. 5.
2. *Metaphysics*, Bk. IV, paragraph 1.
3. John continues: "And the Word was made flesh and dwelt among us: and we saw his glory, the glory as it were of the *only-begotten* of the Father." Jo. i.l. Peter: "Thou art the Christ, the Son of the living God."

ferred to Him as God, Messiah, and Lord. In today's Scriptural reading (Saturday after Easter), for example, the apostles had been performing so many miracles that the scribes hauled these "simple, uneducated men" before the tribunal to shut them up. The apostles said that they would not be silenced by men when they should proclaim that it was in the name of Christ the Lord that these things were done. Eventually they were all martyred defending that view. As Saint John points out in his gospel, the *leaders* of the Jews had Him put to death precisely because He claimed He was God—not the Jewish people, incidentally. Indeed, he cannot be properly evaluated apart from that claim. Conclusion: either He was God, or the greatest of imposters. There can be no in-between logic here.

I cannot believe that you who so often and so affectionately refer to "Our Lord" as well as to Scripture can come to a conclusion in this important matter essentially different from mine. We both like steak "with a bit of fat on the end of it". We both used to say heaven would be ideal if we could eat our steak on the stump of a tree in a garden where you could gather in your plants to your heart's content. I remember the morning when I came in and found you adding up the number of miles you walked in these quests: 3 times around the world. I am not forgetting that you want your own stump. I'm sure "Our Lord" will give it to you, for I cannot believe that anyone who has so ardently, honestly, and for so long pursued the truth, as you have, can miss the green, since God is Truth. Perhaps it is only natural that we should fade the ball around the trees in a different manner, or try to, because I am a left-handed hitter.

In passing, we discussed the work of the philosophers at St. Louis University, in particular that of Henle and Klubertanz, S. J.'s, and James Collins.

April 8, '75

Sheldon took birthday #100 in stride.

I forgot to bring in the report I had written up on our last discussion, but will bring it next time.

This report will be given in three sections:

1. Direct quotations I copied during the course of the discussion. That is, direct quotes of his.
2. A running account of the drift of the discussion.
3. Further discussion of analogy.

I

"I'm getting deafer. I received four or five quarts of whiskey.... One birthday is no different from another, but it happens that 100 is a popular number.... I received 101 cards.... I never was famous...."He was referring to an article in the newspaper from which he felt many had heard of his birthday. He thanked Anne and me over and over for the half-gallon to which we felt he had advanced.

"My great change since my retirement is to the Trinity. I don't think anything in heaven and earth is beyond reason.

"Eventually, we shall live immortally in the flesh. The New Thought held this. Reason is comprehending more and more.

"Reason is timeless.

"Revelation is not against reason.

"Jesus is a man, but endowed with reason."

II

I brought in the Bible and read from St. John where he points out that the reason the leaders of the Jews had Our Lord put to death was because He claimed He was God.

I read further quotes of Jesus' words from St. John which show He indeed made that claim. Sheldon said that was St. John's interpretation, and he was only a man. I said the other writers of the Gospels point out the same facts, and that all of them gave up their lives as martyrs while defending what they proclaimed as truth.

Sheldon said he did not accept the Scriptures and that is why he distinguished between Jesus and the Christ. I had never been aware of this before, that is, that he made this distinction.

He said that he was a rationalist advocating the New Thought view. He said the greatest advance he made since his retirement was to the trinity. Again I said reason can't show why there are three rather than any other number. If he critically examines reason's message it will lead him to the Scriptures which are the source of the three and what three refers to.

We discussed the nature of reason. I said the only conception of reason we know is human reason. He said the angels have reason. I said any further extension of reason was by analogy, and we know about the existence of angels from scripture. He said analogy means identity included, and I said it did not. I shall discuss this in part III.

He said the good was self-realizing, and that is how he comes to the existence of God. I asked him what is the good. All we know are good things. He said the good is related to consciousness, and I agreed.

No doubt, the futility of discussing these matters further at this time was obvious to both of us. Somehow we naturally drifted into a discussion of our foreign policy. Of course, we do not know the inside here. But as philosophers we know the philosophical background of Communism. We compared it to an organism that operates by dividing up and synthesizing states to itself. Hegel's dialectic turned upside down. Unless we are prepared to police the world, which doesn't appreciate what we do anyway, we had better mind our business. What responsibility are other nations taking? As the basis of our foreign policy, we better ask it before we move on each new Communist onslaught. Otherwise, we shall drain ourselves of our youth, money, and prestige. Love gone wrong is very costly. Let us have a foreign policy of questions first, then see what others *do*, before we act.

III

Evidently, my explanation of analogy is not clear. The main point is one cannot manipulate existence. Existence, as far as we can see by our intellects into it, has only a unity of proportionality. One simply has to accept it as it is, when it is, and how it is. Reason has to be allowed to *discover*, not make, the truth if it is to help you.

Analogy simply expresses this proportional unity. This is not an identity that is made by you. That is why analogy is not identity, but a proportion of existence to essence, right down to the individual whom it holds above nothing. Hence, I have existence my way; you have it your way. But I am not you. I have intelligence; God is intelligence. My intelligence is not identical with God's. In other words, existence, intelligence, or anything else are proportionate to the beings who have them.

Existence is proportionate, not identical in you and me. You have your dose of potency, I have mine. Existence has been given to you with your limits; to me with my limits. That is why the only unity existence has is one of proportionality. Analogical knowledge recognizes these proportions —that is what it is for—so that we can see things in their proper perspective.

I do not think you realize that you get, *receive* the truth. *You do not make it.* Contrary to what you say, there is much in heaven and earth beyond reason. Your reason and mine are dosed with potency. God's intelligence is without potency. Consequently, there is no identity between man's reason and God's intelligence—we cannot even talk about them properly in the same terms, and an *equivocal use of the word reason* only makes confused thinking. Between

58

man and God there is only an analogy of proportionality no matter what we are talking about. Therefore you cannot discover the mysteries in His being. He tells you as much as He wishes, simply because He is the First Cause. You must realize you are only a contingent being, consequently reason in you is naturally limited. You must recognize facts, the kind of being you *are*. You must not set up a hypostatized reason that has never existed, identify with it, and judge the truth in the light of it. But that is what you are doing and that is why you cannot discover the true Logos which is "the way, the truth, and the light."

I would not be speaking so sharply to you if I did not think your insight is now as good—I think it is better—as it ever was. You are far from being "over the hill." On the contrary, as you so often say "it is darkest before dawn." I think your insight is reaching out to its true fulfillment in revelation. This hypostatized reason is blocking your vision. Get rid of it. Study analogy; analogy will show you its place. Then you will see revelation is not only "not against reason." It completes *human* reason. Both-and. Accept scripture, the record of revelation, and your insight will see Jesus is the Christ, *both* human *and* Divine.

The unity of proportionality that is being is especially difficult for you to see, because you are used to manipulating ideas. But being is precisely a unity that must be let go. Being, in other words, exists in its own right. You do not make it exist. You must let it be. Then your insight will be freed to expand. Let it follow existence out into each thing that holds existence in its own way. Let it follow existence into the stone, into man, into God. Then you will see the unity of proportionality that is being. This is an entirely different world from a mélange that you make by a unity of equivokes. But it is a true picture of reality.

Reason, like the senses, is only one power, one faculty *by means of which* you and I see, and we are only men. Don't make it the whole program. Pure spirits don't even need it to see.

Professor, your words, the essence of your view, "the timelessness of reason" is the true spirit of St. Thomas. That is why I say you are in spirit one of us without recognizing the fact. You must see, as St. Thomas did, that your reason is reaching out to faith because it has gone as far as it can by itself alone. Your reason must complete itself. Let it go. Your philosophy must fulfill itself in theology to be truly philosophy. Your reason is waiting to see the words of Holy Writ. This is the bank from which your reason has already drawn the blank check of the trinity. Write the names of the three persons on it. Cash it in as the Holy Trinity. Reason needs *your* help, because it is trying to go "forward and upward."

Scripture tells us that the Word, Reason, became flesh in the person of Jesus Christ. No divorce between time and eternity. This is your view, too. In short, the Holy Trinity is grounded in time through the being of Our Lord. I am surprised you don't see this. Power-Love are your ways to represent the other persons. Surely the "only begotten" cannot be divorced from God the Father to whom He always referred. Actually you should be the first to embrace Scripture, because reason has shown you the path all the way.

ANALOGY

St. Thomas presents a beautiful world for contemplation. Supposing we were to enter it, what would I first ask you to do? Put aside the view of analogy as "identity plus added difference," so that Thomism is not twisted in the very attempt to understand it. Then I would say: your existence is yours, my existence is mine, God's existence is His. Surely, we agree on this. That is the basis of analogy. You possess your existence your way, I possess it my way, and God does not need either of us, so He exists as our Creator. Simple, to be sure, but nail it down and apply it. For example.

Since you possess existence your way, I can't have existence—*esse*—as it is in you. Likewise, you can't have my existence. Therefore, there is no identity of existence between us, and to speak of added difference dos not apply. Consequently, if the Thomist is right, this other view of analogy must be rejected.

Another application. Power, reason, and love in like manner exist analogously in each being who has them. Conclusion: each of us—you, I, and God—possess both existence and his attributes in his own way. Therefore, in regard to these attributes there can be no identity between God and man. They are diverse. That is why the Thomist says our knowledge of God is analogous. After all, if He needed us, He would not be our Creator to begin with.

A	exercises its own act of existence	=	the stone
B	"	"	=	"	plant
C	"	"	=	"	Rover
D	"	"	=	"	You
E	"	"	=	Man on Mars
F	"	"	=	Jesus Christ

In short, existence is held by you *in a way* that differs from the way others hold it. Hence the stone is not a man. The only unity between the stone and man is that of proportionality. That is why the energy in the stone is in a solid form, hence stones can't think. But there must be a being who naturally possesses existence, otherwise reason can't account for the *existence* any of these beings have, hence we conclude to God as First Cause: Pure Act, The *Esse*. Thus the *proportionality of existence* is the formal object of metaphysics for the Thomist, because that is as far as the *human* mind can see into it. This is *both* a purely intellectual seeing *and* a limited one.

———————

Reverdy Whitlock had a beautifully engraved scroll drawn up with 100 signatures on it to commemorate Sheldon's birthday, and we enjoyed reading the names of his friends. However, the value of Sheldon's longevity was already achieved some years ago on the day he by-passed Russell. He never could swallow Russell, either from a philosophical or personality standpoint. I remember saying, "Well, you are now the only philosopher in captivity who has outlived that hen-pecked old bird."

Since Sheldon's vision and hearing could be better, he prefers not to read books and articles, but rather bits that I might write on subjects we are discussing, hence they are included in what follows. Besides, it cuts down on the shouting and the ladies will not think we are fighting when we are just trying to get through the sound barrier. Of course, we fight, too, but no that loud. How else does one recycle his energy? He is always gentle and firm and I try to emulate him. He never adds that humiliating nudge that would push one into the brink.

April 15, '75

When I came in, Sheldon kindly said: "Your argument for immortality should be put into a big volume. It is an enormously important argument. We are rational beings. We are timeless so far. I feel that strongly. That book of mine was over 700 pages. If you make it a big book, it will appeal to the scientific type of mind."

Here he was referring to his *God and Polarity*.

I said that right now my thoughts were centered on trying to show how his inclusive point of view—both-and—naturally coincides with the Thomist point of view, if both-and were seen in the light of *esse*. Their view of analogy is based on *esse*. So I wrote out a little stint on *esse* which I would like to read today.

During the course of our discussion, William James's name came up. Sheldon said he did a lot of work with him and Royce, that he met James's wife, she approved of "my make-up, and invited me to dinner. James is a bright writer, warm hearted. His pupils loved him. But he isn't much of a thinker. He is a feeler. He argues you to have an open mind, but he doesn't bother to think often. Royce goes beyond, but he doesn't have that bright way. Royce is a philosopher. He emphasizes reason, but not feeling enough."

Let me present now my little essay on *esse*, and follow it with the main point you stressed during the discussion.

ESSE: Existential Act

There is no part of existence that is not existence.

Existence is proportioned in two directions, horizontally and vertically. Both-And.

If one attempts to grasp it *exclusively* in either one or the other, it is split and lost. It must be seen in its essential proportionality; otherwise it is not authentic.

Existence is not exclusively held in time. It cannot, in other words, be held exclusively in essence. That is why the mind cannot hold it in a concept. It spills over into another concept, then another, then another, on and on. That is the horizontal direction of existence. But what is the condition of the possibility of its horizontal direction? Its vertical proportionality. Both-and.

It—existence—could not be held in this essence, that essence, and still another essence, if it did not transcend all essences. They limit it to this or that. But existence itself transcends all genera. Therefore, vertically it is proportioned to Pure Act.

Because of this essential proportionality of existence, it is *both* limited in essence, in time, and unlimited in eternity, in Pure Act.

Pure Act therefore Causes existence to be put into essence proportionally as it sees fit. In other words existence is proportioned to time, and this is what we mean by creation. (vertical proportionality)

But then the creator lets the individual so formed from essence and existence take over. X becomes a creator, because he has participated in vertical causality as its term *ad quem*. From this he creates or causes further creations. (horizontal proportionality)

This is the Divine plan, existentially presented. The great danger in it is that man does not see that existence is simply proportioned in him. He thinks that because he has been given the power to create, he is the sole creator. He loses sight of the vertical proportionality of existence which is the condition of his possibility. God did not have to permit Existence to be constitutive or proportioned to him. Existence is constitutive of him in time, but it is not limited to essence. Its simplicity cannot be grasped in temporal molds.

Man can see the proportionality and directions of existence. But he does not make the proportions. If he thinks he can, he is left with mere empty essences to manipulate in his limited mind. Reason is a tool in the service of life of the mind. But if it becomes enamored with its own operation, the life of the mind is enslaved. What has reason that the essence of man has not given it? What has essence that the Pure Act has not given to it in existence? In short, man's exclusiveness causes his fall. That is why God became man to restore his vision.

Indeed, your view is the best way to get my view through. Paradoxically, I cannot get through to you. The essential proportionality of *esse* is the answer. It is proportioned to you in one way in me another way. That is why we are both free.

During the discussion today Sheldon said, "I can't read more than a few hours a day."

Then he said: "If you are a perfect rationalist, reason implies the possibility of more and more. The old view was the more we know, the more certain we are. Now the more we know, the more opportunities are open to us. Immortality is an indefinitely long ability to see there is more to be seen. Reality is infinite. God is infinite. He can do anything. The more we progress, the nearer we come to the Divine nature. Think of the infinite number of machines we can make, the number of puzzles we discover. (He is fond of doing crossword puzzles). We must understand what growth means. Don't limit the self to a fixed nature. We must become aware that our religions have been very limited. The church decided what we must do. That is literally bringing up a child. But we do it less and less as he grows older, especially your church. As it progresses it learns we discover new things. Most Christian churches don't believe in progress. Only the Unitarian believed in progress.

"But it is wrong to think reason is cold. Reason implies love, because it includes the many in one. It really doesn't deny the many. Reason implies value, because it is beautiful in itself. What is more beautiful than the organic structure of arithmetic? Reason is orderly, and order is beautiful. That is why one person of the trinity implies the other. Reason implies beauty and power to love and express. The trinity is a beautiful doctrine. The parts join together in a beautiful union."

APRIL 22, '75

When I sat beside him, Sheldon said he had his favorite breakfast this morning: corned beef and cabbage. He said that has always been his favorite dish since his youth.

I said that I had gone to the stacks in the library to find a work on energy, but by chance I came upon a splendid work by a nun, Sister John, which gives the views of a number of Thomists, the thread of union of the essays being, of course, *esse*.[1]

Sheldon repeated his view of chance which is the same as mine and given elsewhere in these discussions. Then he added that the Good Lord put the book into my hands. We say I came upon it by chance, but the substructure is the Divine Causality.

From the book we read and discussed many passages from Father Fabro's clearly expressed view. My little stint above on *esse* was inspired by what he said about vertical and horizontal causality. I had often thought along those lines.

During the course of the discussion, Sheldon asked what the author's view was. I replied that she did not give her own view. There is no commenting summary or chapter giving her view. He said that was typical of woman and shows their great admiration for individual persons.

He did not use the word men referring to persons, so far as I recall, but I shall take the responsibility of adding it, and I think he would agree. We did not say that women are not original thinkers—we know where our corned beef and cabbage comes from. This work is a typical example that they are exact, clear, precise, reliable, beautiful scholars.

I try to get down as much as I can of what Sheldon says. I don't like to interrupt him, because of the beauty of his discourse which is captivating, but he talks as if he were

---

1. *The Thomist Spectrum.* (Fordham U. Press, N.Y., '66).

reading it, and he makes many connections with twists and turns which I often miss. He began here to talk about time:

"Reason is timeless. God Himself is timeless. Where does time come from? Reason doesn't imply it. Answer: there is another factor that reason includes, the love factor.

"Why does God create time? So that in time there would be different moments. He created different elements so they would develop in time. He created something that is the object of love.

"Time is the way many small things grow and come nearer the fullness of being. He created time so that the love motive would show itself. His love is so great He creates these smaller beings. He makes these smaller beings so that they could improve.

"There comes in the beauty of human love. God gave man a time sense so that he would know what it is to get better and better. It is the love motive.

"Reason has a beauty of its own. Reason includes love in its structure. Each part helps another to be. That makes a different event for each one, hence time. This being includes another and another.

"God creates time to give things he created the joy of including more and more. Time is due to the love motive including reason: one part including another and another. Time is separate events, the joy of one step added to another, not a still eternity.

"Reason is inclusive. The trouble with Christianity is the love motive is taken as distinct from reason. But it includes reason. Reason would not be reason without love. It is a polarity. No exclusions. Both-And. Devotion to one does not exclude devotion to the other.

"The application of this to the trinity has not been seen. It is illustrated in many different ways. With us, man, woman—the application of power: love. She brings up the child, sees what is good for the child. Then comes the emancipation of woman, the second stage. The third stage is coming forth in a wild form, the emancipation of the young. First, power, in Christianity: behave and you'll go to heaven. The motive of love was not stressed. Be baptized and you'll go to heaven. No love motive. This is not the way Jesus lived. He helped the multitude, healed disease, fed the multitude. That is the essence of Christianity. It is the love religion. The third step is not as intelligent as it should be. A new movement begins in the wrong direction. Religion began in the wrong direction, mysticism, getting away from the world. Christianity brought it back, making it broader. But Christianity got exclusive, accepting certain dogmas, not what Jesus taught, rather what the church adopted. I felt that and never joined any sect. A new movement begins with mistakes. They are in the power stage. They will come to the rational stage, and then will enter the love motive. Love comes in through reason. What you want is to make things better."

APRIL 29, '75

When I entered, Sheldon showed me a Japanese pipe he received from one of his Japanese students by the name of Miss Shena Kan.

Then he began immediately to say, "We men have fixed ideas. Never stop using reason, though we have faith. In my little book *Rational Religion,* I say that confidence is based on experience. It helps you to keep going."

J: I agree.

S: We agree fundamentally. Faith does not abolish reason. Faith is a stimulus. I believe certain things I don't understand yet. We think reason has absolutely demonstrated something, but it has not demonstrated all about it. All bodies feel gravitation, but we have the ability to turn it aside and let other forces act. We can stop gravitation when we hold up an object. We don't destroy gravitation, but we hold it up, and may do so by spiritual powers. There is no gulf between the spirit world and this world. There is a distance."

J: I can agree with everything you say. But there is one more thing about faith. It adds something of its own that reason can't discover. For example, by reason we prove the existence of a First Cause who is Pure Act, God. But then He tells you things about Himself you can't discover by reason.

S: Reason by itself. No. Like married life. Man can do lots of things. But with woman's help he can do more. She stands for Divine things. Exclusion is the source of all evil. That is why God gave us time.

J: Yes, there are two causal lines. Vertical, from God to man; horizontal, man's causality in time. We should not disjunct these energies.

S: Christians take faith exclusively.

69

J: Maybe some do, but that is not the Catholic, nor St. Thomas's view.

S: The trouble is that people think you take certain doctrines and that is enough. But that is not the emphasis in Thomism. The Thomist upholds freedom. Certain Christians taught to forget the self. No, there is no love without the self that loves. The self both exists by itself and with something else. Exclusion is the root of all evil. Faith means I do think I am going to succeed eventually. God gave us sleep to gather strength to do work. Apparently sleep is an exclusive activity. But no. It welcomes its bride, the marriage of sleep and work.

The thing I want to stress is, according to the teaching of Jesus, the center of the good life is here. Develop the power God gave us to enjoy the fullness of existence here and now. Here and now. Every statement of Jesus is centered on the good physical life now. Bring physical happiness to everyone. He cured disease, gave food to the multitude, so they could keep living. He resurrected Lazarus to life. The sister of Lazarus said: "Lord, if you were here, my brother would not have died." She feels with feminine instinct that we should have the good life now. This does not mean to exclude the joy of heaven. But God made matter. Smoke your pipe. Drink your liquor, seeing you don't drink too much.

J: Yes, that's why you used to have that elastic around your glass. You used to measure it by your fingers against your stomach. Four fingers up.

S: Exclusion of the physical—that is the great curse. Religion has not centered on this. It has centered on the future. But you must enjoy things here. What God made is good if we use it not to exclude. If there is anything bad, it is the prohibitionist. Jesus said, "Unless you become as little children," because little children enjoy good things by experiment. Youth is venturesome. This does not mean do anything you want. But don't neglect the body. Cultivate it to include other goods. That's why sex, properly used, is heavenly. Woman knows that in her heart. Sex is central. Without it there would be no life on earth. But how many have

70

emphasized celibacy? This is not good unless necessary in some particular case.

Jesus' last message was a banquet, to feed them. He loved matter. He made it divine. He saved His own life. His body remained. He didn't say to Lazarus's sister, "Cheer up, he's gone to heaven." He reunited him to the body. Jesus stands for the inclusion of life by infusion of the spirit. Jesus taught bringing of the spirit into the body—mountains, trees, rivers, the beautiful ocean with its beautiful waves. Jesus loved matter—the wedding of spirit and matter, not the life of spirit alone. Have the churches realized that His last act was a supper. The body is good if it is not used to hurt other bodies. Infuse the body with spirit and it is most beautiful. There is heaven on earth if you only knew it. Life should continue.

The atonement is interpreted as if Jesus gave up in pain and nothing else. But he overcame pain. "It is finished. Father, to thee I give my soul." That statement doesn't mean it is the end. It means He overcame. It makes the body, spirit—consummated. His body didn't remain in the tomb. It was realized, verified by the ladies. He revealed it first to women. Women are nearer to seeing fundamental truths.

J: Ms. would like to hear that.

S: We make woman the emotional one; man, the scientist. There is no such gulf. There is the fundamental beauty of sex. Sex is taken to be mere bodily lust. But it is the holy union of spirit and body. It is no longer lust; it is love. Sex love is not a spasm. In the love of husband and wife, it is a blissful union. It is not a seizure as it is with the animal. Sex love is taken as material. But the beauty of sex is that it is an extension of Divine love. Man and woman combine: the trinity—Power, Intellect, Love, man woman, child. Polarity is unity as well as duality. Man, woman, in their union a new life is born, the child. The trinity is realized everywhere if we but knew it. It is not just a doctrine of faith. Most Christians misunderstand it, that it is a matter of faith only —they should see that it is a teaching on the level of science. It is wrong to separate faith and reason.

71

The trinity is the most important idea, not just in man. It is the marriage of duality. Love is the union of power and intelligence. Reason includes love, because reason is a system. And we love it. We must show reason includes love and love includes reason. All bound together. Most Christians haven't seen this. They think reason is the lowest stage. But the logic of the whole thing is beautiful. The Trinity brings this out.

MAY 6, '75

I mentioned to Sheldon that I met Harrison, the Librarian, and he sent his regards. "He especially enjoyed reading in *The New Haven Register* about those hearty breakfasts you have."

S: He is always a bright, cheerful person. I had a beautiful breakfast today, scrambled eggs.

J: That's a tid-bit for you.

S: My digestion was off a bit last night. What is that big book you have?

I showed him a bound volume of *The International Philosophical Quarterly* in which I was reading an article by Coreth, Professor of Philosophy at Innsbrück, entitled "The Problem and Method of Metaphysics."

S: Method in metaphysics. I always find fault with method. Subjective: doesn't get out of the subjective world. That isn't metaphysics.

J: He would agree with you. He is trying to meet modern thought on its own grounds—the whole essentialist line.

S: Method is like trying to cure yourself before taking the doctor's medicine. Just go ahead, explain reality.

J: He follows in the Maréchal movement. By means of a transcendental deduction he shows that metaphysics of being is the condition of the possibility of asking questions.

We read together several passages from Coreth's article which traces the development of modern thought and shows it is essentialist in spirit about as clearly as I have ever seen it done. Sheldon has a unique and characteristic way of taking each sentence apart and rephrasing it to express it from out of the framework of his own system. We went so rapidly, it was difficult to take notes, and I can't rephrase his inimitable style. To be fair to him, I confess I am never sure I get him right, yet he never complains.

I then read some passages from Raemaeker which stress that the formal object of metaphysics is *esse*. He does a beautiful job.

As I type this out, I might add that it is good with Coreth to show the conditions of the possibility—providing one first understands that *esse* is proportionate. Of course he comes to the job equiped with this knowledge. But does the modern philosopher have the slightest idea of *esse?* That is truly another world. For *Coreth,* O.K.

Esse must not be confused with things or essence. It must be seen in its own light—proportionality. Everything turns on not converting this vision into a dialectic of essences. *Esse* cannot be manipulated by the concepts of man. But divorced from being by Descartes, philosophy followed the line of essence by manipulation to Hegel, then to Marx, who turned it upside down to pervade the practical order to the conquest of Vietnam. And now to the conquest of Europe in ten years, as Kissinger rightly pointed out last night. Are we next? Just look at what is going on here. No, the fall is not ended yet. Man's mis-use of freedom makes nonbeing. This was the theme of my *March Toward Matter* many years ago. Just the names and the dates need to be filled in.

However, as you often say, "It is darkest before dawn." God is good and all-powerful. Man is free; he can still look up. And also, as you so often say, "America has a big heart." Look at the way we take these refugees in when we are in a depression ourselves. He might not want us to fall. We are not prophets. We don't know the Divine plan. We must hope for the best, work and pray for it. Still, the fall is not just a religious myth, but deeply a guide to the destiny of man. "So far," as you say, he is still falling—Vietnam.

Sheldon said at one point in our discussion, "My eyes are not so good. It takes time for them to wake up. That prevents me from helping you as I should."

I replied, "Your insight is stronger than it ever was."

He admitted that he sees many more new things now. He has already written two books in the '90's.

I said, "You are the living proof of your friend, Sinnott's view and, incidentally, I ran across a passage in *Contra Gentiles* where St. Thomas says the same thing: the mind gets weaker in those aspects where it is dependent on the body, e.g., the memory of names; it gets stronger, however, in those respects where it operates on its own, e.g., insights, synthesizing ideas in new ways. As people get older, they become embarrassed when they cannot remember a name, but they don't take account of the ways in which they have advanced."

Sheldon: Both-And—if you mentioned both-and in my early days, I wouldn't have appreciated it.

J: The rational energy system that is you and I is both dependent on the environment as the source of its energy, food, the sun's rays, etc., and independent of the environment in its manner of operation—naturally, because it has its own being, like any of the other 92+ elements. Naturally, this both-and is reflected in our beings.

It is strange how prejudice and ignorance combine to prevent progress. There are new emergents at every level in nature that you cannot account for on the basis of the level below, otherwise they would not be new levels, e.g., the wetness of water cannot be seen in either hydrogen or oxygen. But people do not realize that the rational energy system also has its own contribution to make. We see the transformations it makes in the environment all around us by means of its abstract ideas, its creative power. Do the dogs and cats do these things; do they go to work; do they make atom bombs which in the end may even blow themselves up? Yet we do not specifically distinguish the power of life in a man from the life in a cat; consequently, death in one case has no more significance than death in the other.

Death like life is an analogous concept. The life span of a rose is the summer, of a dog about fifteen years, of a man —except Sheldon—about four score and ten. And life must not be restricted to exclusively earthly conditions. Life is bound up with the cosmic conditions where it is realized. On more distant planets, life might very well be measured in terms of light years. In the lab now the conditions are realized to convert the energy of matter into light. Energy actually exists in this condition on other planets. Why not life? Analogously, then, the role of death will be different there. Its role is proportionate to what is, not to what is not, for we know what is not from what is, as Aristotle said long ago. On these planets, life might be evolved from an element other than carbon, for example, hence the configuration of the body would be different, the remains would be different, in short, there would not be so much otherness to overcome. Perhaps on another planet, however, there would be more otherness to overcome. Depending on conditions, then, on some planets death would be more smooth, a gradual transition, and perhaps a pleasure, like any change for the better. 21st Century microphysics will know much more about the conditions in other galaxies, even as it works here in the lab, and this will be the basis for broader knowledge of life and, when we update our thinking, consequently of the material essence of death. But we have to take on the cosmic perspective of energy, conceive it in an analogical frame-work and stop thinking in these fixed, earthly molds. To a being on some other planet, death as we know it might be as unintelligible to him as life on his planet is at present unintelligible to us.

Perhaps we should not be talking about communication between planets. Right here on ours, the lack of communication between the old and the new is the tragedy of the intellectual world. Young people today are almost ignorant of their heritage, because it is not passed on to them. Even in great thinkers like Dewey, for example, we find him opposing the "fixed" view of substance, and he calls this the Aristotelian view. Whereas Aristotle opposes this view as strongly as Dewey. This rift is now appearing in the practical order. It is called the generation gap.

MAY 13, '75

As soon as I was seated, Sheldon said:

"You might emphasize the difference between man and woman. All depends on the union of the two. Emphasize the distinction.

"Woman loves the individual. Man loves the universal. Woman loves *esse*. Man is *essentia*. Man is better fitted to the public life and laws. Woman loves individuals and wants to see that they are taken care of.

"All this protest of woman is not directly connected with law.

"No metaphysic can be broad enough that doesn't emphasize difference. Woman's protest went to extreme. Some women do excellent work in public life, but woman as a rule wants a family and child, but not public life.

"Man wants to frame laws. Neither excludes the other, but they differ. It takes two. 1&2, and then a separate number, 3. Man, woman-child. Hence the family is an example of the trinity. Man (power) woman (intelligence) and child (love). Trouble is the trinity is confined to God."

Sheldon concluded, "That is my lecture for today." He also urged that these ideas be included in this work.

We have gone over this ground many times before, but, perhaps as I type this out, we can recycle our energy again in a new way. There is no question that the human family is a beautiful analogy to the Divine family. No doubt, the First Cause leaves His impression on His effects, "so far," we should add, as space and time permit and human reason can see, being itself before Divine things as limited "as the eye of the bat before the noon-day sun."

In what follows I would like to concentrate more on the

broader relationship of Thomism and Modern Thought than our relationship, although we are good examples of how much fun and even how valuable such rapprochement can be. In many respects philosophy is much like chess, serious fun. Well, you were once engaged in a series of articles in *The Modern Schoolman* with Maritain, and I did enjoy them, because you taught me so much about Thomism. You were sharp then and even sharper now. You are like an electron; reach for you here and you are there. I have to watch you and be very careful, or I shall lose my Queen, so I'm going to move my pawn in front of her here—just in case. You say here, "Woman loves *esse*. Man is *essentia*." Well, this could be said either from ignorance—which in your case I doubt very much, indeed. Or it could be said to reduce what I regard as the formal object of metaphysics to the level of the being of daily life, being in the world, *dasein*. In other words, the *unity of proportionality* vital to *esse* as the subject of metaphysics, as I understand it, is *split* up by you between the sexes. This is both check and mate, if I allow it to happen. For existential act, *esse*, which makes each thing be, real or possible, cannot be proportioned at all if man is essence, and *esse* is turned over to the ladies. There is, however, a third possibility. As so often happens, what you mean here might be sailing right over my head. In that case, just regard what I said as an introduction to a few comments on the relation of Thomism to Modern Thought.

The trouble with communication here is there is so much training required—for example, just in the matter of making distinctions, ontology, that present-day thought has been cut off from for so long—before one gets to *esse*, that it is practically impossible to get through to the modern philosopher on the need for and the value of metaphysics as a science with its own formal object, *esse*, and that if you see things in this light, you get a whole new slant on things. I don't blame him for thinking we are out of it, and I don't mean this in a bad sense: that this is a world he knows nothing about. This is and has been the situation for a long time—two different worlds. For rapprochement purposes, both can live if they recognize that knowledge is *both* of *being* in the world, things we see every day, *and* *esse*, the existential act which holds them above nothing or they wouldn't *be* at all. As you say, exclusion is the root of all evil. If, however, concepts are limited to their possible empirical use, then *esse*, the science of metaphysics as we understand it is out. But then, so is intelligence, for what good is it if we cannot see more by means of it than we can by the senses alone? But as a simple matter of fact, the condition of the possibility of perceiving this particular thing is that it first exists. But this particular thing cannot exclusively hold *esse*, the act of existence, for there is another thing that has it, still another, and another. In short, precisely because we are intelligent, we can see this transcendental act which is the condition of the possibility of each being in the world, hence the necessity of admitting *esse*, the formal object of the science of metaphysics. Moreover, since the senses are needed on the side of th object, to bring us into contact with the environment, if the environment is different on some other planet, the senses of intelligent life there might be different from ours, yet these beings might be more advanced in knowledge. Maybe that's why they don't want to get in touch with us yet, or, never, so long as we remain savages, so long as we nail intelligence down to this earth.

MAY 20, '75

I brought in an article on the *Human Body,* because I know you are interested in this subject.[1]

This prompted you to say:

"In Jesus when on earth mind and body were fully united. Christianity separated mind and body. In Jesus spirit and body are one. Jesus was the second person in the body, and when He died the body continued."

"You won't be willing to admit this, but I don't believe His death was a sacrifice. It was a resurrection. But He resurrected His body for our vision, to prepare the way, making our body more spiritual, life on earth, heavenly life in the flesh."

I would have to comment on these statements one at a time.

1. Christianity separated mind and body.

Comment. The Catholic Church has always promulgated the resurrection of the body as an article of faith.

2. Your concluding sentence in paragraph one.

Comment. True. That is precisely what I have been arguing for in the Trinity.

3. Paragraph two: "You won't be willing", etc.

Comment. Most authorities would say you are being exclusive here. Christ's coming here, His suffering and death on the cross are both a sacrifice and a demonstration that the body is resurrected after death. No doubt, your reason is trying to show you that you should accept scripture, because *your argument is based on it.* But it is a *nonsequitur* to conclude from any of this that there will be some sort of heavenly life in the flesh on earth.

---

1. A splendid article by Hengstenberg in one of the early issues of The *International Philosophical Quarterly.*

Concerning speculations about future life on earth, one must recognize that today atomic power is steadily increasing in multiples of ten times the power of the atom bomb. Aside from the power of the Creator to destroy the world whenever He wants to as a possibility, man now has the power to destroy humanity himself. Nations recognize the concern of the scientists over man's precarious situaton which is getting worse, and so should we. However, if one does not think of life in terms of its confinement to earthly conditions, there is no need to get "up-tight" about these additional *conditions* either.

No doubt you and I could agree on Teilhard's emphasis on the pleroma at the end. We have discussed this before— the union of the quantitative and qualitative in God.

May 27, '75

I came in with several ideas that occurred to me on the value of conversation. I had them written down and suggested that we might use them as the basis of our discussion. I said that we are a good example of the value of this technique. We go on and on and yet we don't have to agree. "And the important result is I am always learning from you."

S: New ideas keep coming in. For example I have a new idea. On the face of it it sounds ridiculous. There are analogies to the trinity all through. This seems forced.

J: Go ahead and present it.

S: This seems forced. But consider the human face, just the face: the external organs are the eye, the nose, the mouth. Let me show you the analogy. With the eye we get light; it goes with knowledge. The basis of knowledge is reason. God said: "Let there be light." Light gives us understanding.

The nose—very ridiculous again but through the nose we breathe. Breath is the source of life, gives us air. In matter—the energy of light, air.

The third organ, the mouth. Through the mouth we get food, and food is the source of continued life and is matter, even liquid food is matter.

Those are the fundamental facial organs. The eye gives light and is *reason*. Air—life, life gives *power*. Every living thing has some power.

The analogy, then, *reason, power*. The food we get we enjoy. We *love* it. If we didn't like our food, we wouldn't take it. All this is bodily energy. Food is a fundamental enjoyment of consciousness.

(Sheldon has here been presenting his conception of the trinity in terms of Power, Reason, and Love which we have considered more in detail before.)

J: This is a beautiful analogy. How clear your mind works. No notes, just like reading it from a script.

S: And God said, "Let there be light." Let it be seen when consciousness comes along, hence reason. Yes, that is interesting. Too bad the Unitarian missed all that, because he missed its meaning.

(As I type this out, however, I would have to say in defense of the Unitarian that he is perfectly consistent, because from the point of view of reason alone, one cannot see how the being of Trinity is involved.)

J: I have been reading an article in which the writer contrasts the specific differences between man and the animals. The animal's face is expressionless, but man's countenance shows his spirit: joy, sadness, the quizzical look, etc. In my framework, no one organ expresses the whole countenance: we can't see the Godhead in each of the three persons.

S: The organic unity reveals the character of the person who owns it. We judge the person's nature by looking at it. There are three distinct parts.

As I type this out, these ideas came to mind as I try to see your beautiful analogy in our framework. We might say there are *two* aspects in the trinity—energy is polarized.[1] The Godhead is *The Esse*, in Gilson's terminology. We arrive at it by reason *via* the First Cause, hence Pure Act. Also, the three distinct persons which we get from Scripture: Christ said, "I am in the Father, and the Father is in me.... Now I go the Father, and I will send the Paraclete, the Holy Spirit." By synthesizing reason and faith, then, in the light of your analogy: the countenance—face— is the Godhead. The eyes are reason, the Son; nose, the Holy Spirit—breath; the mouth, energy, the Father. We must conserve *both* the Godhead *and* the three persons; otherwise we have only three persons or attributes, as you put it, which are empty of being. Your reason is trying to show you it needs Scripture, for it is only one power in a

1. Sheldon's massive work: *God and Polarity*. (Yale U. Press)

limited human being. It relies on the words of God which Scripture provides to cope with these Divine matters. As a matter of fact you are quoting from Scripture all the time. Even above you quoted twice from *Genesis*. You said, "God said, 'Let there be light'." When an athlete plays a game, there is a rule book behind it, and he must acknowledge the fact.

We then turned to the points on conversation which I had written down. I shall summarize Sheldon's comments on these.

1. Conversation is a natural way to recycle rational energy toward reality. This recycling eliminates subjectivism.

S: I never like the word recycling. The word cycle puzzles me. (C. F., the conversation of March 23.)

2. Conversation takes us out of ourselves and our exclusive hold on essences.

S: Yes, that's a big point. That's the only thing that saved me growing up. When I had conversations I learned something. I got the last idea talking with you. Man can't exist and think alone. If thoughts are shared, they are intelligible. That's where the beauty of difference comes in. Different as we are, we see some truth, if the conversation is rightly conducted.

3. Each word, each question by the other person causes us to recycle our energy, critically examine ourselves. Ideas are not exclusively ours. These ideas are founded on existence.

S: We must converse or ideas will die. The beauty of writing 'em out is for others to see them. The one needs the many and the many become one if they agree. We agree fundamentally, because we see the truth.

4. Dictators don't like conversation. They stifle questions. Nicholas of Russia wouldn't listen, hence the revolutionfl. Marx was just as much of a dictator. He stifled questions. They don't want to see reality but have an exclusive hold on essences.

S: "Of course. Quite right. If you deny conversation, you deny intelligence. In Communism the ruling class tells what is good. It's better than tyranny. That's why Russia made progress over Czarism. That's the trouble with authority. That's what the Unitarian felt against dogma. We need doctrine. Authority? We must believe."

Here I replied that there is no coersion if we accept the authority as the truth as the Christian accepts Scripture, which is, of course, the basis of our doctrine.

As I type this out, I might add that one Sunday I saw the Boston-Washington game in the semi-finals of the N.B.A. If the referee were not there to enforce the rules, that game would indeed have been organized mayhem. In like manner, Scripture needs the Church. The rules do not enforce themselves. Is this tyranny? No. *If* one wants to play the game, he *must* respect the rules; otherwise, the referee calls fouls and can throw the player out, if necessary. Of course, the referee makes mistakes, and so does the Church being run by human beings like you and me. But the players showed great respect for the referee's authority precisely because he was very strict at the beginning of the game. They got the message; they knew they could not run that ball game; otherwise, five feet eleven Kevin Porter would have been killed by those six-feet eight monsters. *If* we want to probe into Divine matters, Jesus Christ came here precisely to give us the rule book to guide us, simply because human reason does not see God. And it is good to have a Church to enforce these limits, protect the rules of the game, because the little man has a right to play without being molested. And who among us is not a little man? Only one, Jesus Christ, because He was *both* man *and* God. He alone has the right to be both player and give the rule book. You and I are only players. Scripture: "Only one is the teacher; the rest, learners."

5. Conversation is based on the proportionality of existence. The participants are free. It gives them the opportunity to see existence together, but they don't have to agree.

S: Yes.

6. Each conclusion in a conversation holds the potential point of departure for a new go-round. As I said, this is the natural way to recycle rational energy. The end is the beginning for a new reflection. That's what Aristotle pointed out in the *De Anima* as *the* specific difference of the life of the mind from material activity which ends outside.

S: We learn by conversation. We get new ideas. You give me new ideas. Latent in me, but you bring them out. This is what conversation can bring about. Conversation: turning about together.

7. Conversation is the natural way for the life of the mind to overcome otherness. The mind has to die to itself to live a new life when it converses with another.

S: I think your ideas, not my own, temporarily, of course. The self energizes the self by being with the other. We are not exclusive. Exclusion is the root of all evil.

8. Conversation shows the vitality of rational energy. It both goes out and returns to itself with a complete return. Material acts just go out, produce otherness, do not conquer it.

S: Conversation is necessary in the pursuit of truth. That is why it is right to publish. Conversation goes further than any one thesis. If the writer of a book could talk to those who read it, he'd learn something more. I've always learned something from readers. I see why they disagree and the cause.

As the ladies entered, we began to discuss the following: Conversations and transcendental deductions are valuable for us, but they do not *add* any *thing* to being.

June 3, '75

As soon as I was seated, Sheldon said: "I'm more convinced than ever we meet reality by doing something. Thought coupled with deed gives salvation. You show it by your writing, by helping others. We always live by action. It takes will to make us think. It's both-and. Not mere action. Nothing is good by itself alone. Everything needs a companion. Those philosophies just based on thought alone won't help. A pure mystical or monistic view, this and this alone gives you final truth, cannot be accepted. Dualism is right. This means the trinity. This, that, and their union. Love and intelligence united in action. Yes. The poor Unitarian did not understand the meaning of the trinity. He is right so far as he reveres reason, but reason needs revelation. There dawns on us a new thought. That has been my experience and yours."

At another time, he said: "There is no exclusion between love and reason. We love this person. Love includes intelligence. Marriage—each needs the other, even if it does not fulfill his own needs. The trouble is we embody our philosophy in a group of men who have a creed. No exclusion."

At another time, he said: "Both-and. If we could only get people to understand the value of that. We must have faith in things we don't understand. We shall come to see why. We have to accept things on faith in this life. But we are coming to understand them more and more. After all, it's faith and reason. We must not take reason in an exclusive sense. God is pure reason, but reason includes love and power. The trinity is the most beautiful doctrine taught by Christianity. Christianity is better, because more inclusive."

Perhaps the main thing I said during the course of the discussion was that faith includes God's word, revelation.

87

For this communication between us and God, analogy is needed. Christ said: "I am in the father, and the father is in me."

Indeed, between my father and me, I can understand the relation of filiation, but we are not in each other. Hence being is attributed to God and man analogously. Sheldon replied, "Analogy is needed in this life, but we are coming to understand more and more."

I said: "That's why St. Thomas looked forward to the Beatific Vision, because it is 'face to face'."

As I type this out, the following thoughts come to view. The more I discuss with you, the more I feel it is too bad you could not have discussed with a more sympathetic type of thinking like Teilhard or a Richard St. Victor. All three of you have a kind of mystical insight which baffles me. I want to know which tree makes shingles, and you keep showing me all the trees.

I need technical terms to see, whereas you want everything on the level of common sense. Most of the articles I give you, you return with the comment, "Not clear, too technical." In effect, this amounts to rejecting the whole science of metaphysics, as the Aristotelians understand it, for if you take away the surgeon's instruments, he cannot operate. To the extent that he needs them to operate, he is, of course, exclusive.

You and Teilhard look to the future a great deal. He looks forward to the merging of science and religion. I'm sure you, too, like this, because it is actually your view. No doubt, both of you here put your finger on a way to get through to modern thought. But I'm sorry, I can't think in the light of a hope for the future which I do not know. Like you, Teilhard avoids metaphysics as a science with its own *formal* object—without which there could be no science of anything. He never mentions St. Thomas—in anything I ever read, and you and I read much of him together. For both of you there is this dynamic surge forward. You see out of this framework of future inclusiveness, whereas I need the instruments that have been sharpened up since the time of Aristotle: organized, systematized science. Religion? I go to church in the morning. Then there is metaphysics; then there is also golf in the P.M. But I do not pray as I hit the ball. Maybe after, as my ball sails toward the brink. But no mélange. Each thing in its time and place, just as each science has its own formal object and its own technical terms. The scientist as a scientist does not worship God; to be a good scientist all he has to do is seek the truth as it is shown to him from the aspect of being he investigates.

I am identifying the difference in spirit between us. I brought in this article by Hengstenberg on the phenomenology of the body, because you like to stress matter and the body. "Not clear, too technical," you said. Perhaps it was unkind of me to try to give you a dose of it again, but I was fascinated by the technical analyses which showed how unintelligible matter is without its relation to existence as he drew the results of micro-physics into the body. How can one talk about matter and the body if he does not get into these technical matters?

You should like Rahner. He includes this dynamic side in religion, yet without the mystic element you and Teilhard have: man works out his salvation dynamically in time. So, I brought a generally recognized outstanding article by McCool on Rahner. "Not clear." You want it on the level of common sense, no doubt. But you can't see *esse* on this level. That's why metaphysics is a science. I pursue this. You say I'm exclusive.

Perhaps, because you are over 100, I should excuse you from reading technical works. I do not. I know better than trying to play you by giving you a few strokes at the outset. Incidentally, of late I have noticed that you can't hear my strong arguments, but when I bring forth a weak one, I find myself trying to pull myself "Off the ropes."

Richard St. Victor is a mystic. Like you, a trinitarian. Like you, pragmatic. He stresses experiment in your sense, spiritual experiment. You both have this mystical drive, and you both use a dialectic to get it out. You nod in the direction of disciplined thought and keep going. You want to communicate a personal, practical experience on the level of daily life and include everything in the dialectical march —a work of love, no doubt about it, that culminates in what is generally recognized as the most inclusive philosophical mansion an American philosopher has yet built.[1] No doubt, these conversations could be put into a little room in the attic, but keep the door open.

As Anne and Nancy entered today, I tried to get down what you said in an off-hand comment, but I can't make out my abbreviations. I don't want to misquote you here, so correct me, if necessary: "My reason does not prove the Trinity. I have the feeling it is right. I say the mystical can be explained. Faith is included. We need faith. We can't help accepting reason. I don't accept faith as fundamental doctrine, that's all."

I think you are a Christian mystic philosopher. You are trying to express by reason the truth of the Trinity that the Holy Spirit has impressed in your heart.

"So Far"

---

1. The last chapter in Y. Krikorian's splendid *Recent Perspectives in American Philosophy* is a capital presentation of Sheldon's view.